DESPERATE

woman

SEEKS

FRIENDS

REAL TALK ABOUT CONNECTION, REJECTION, AND TRYING AGAIN FOR THE FRIENDSHIPS YOU NEED

Kristen Strong

W PUBLISHING GROUP

AN IMPRINT OF THOMAS NELSON

Published in Nashville, Tennessee, by W Publishing, an imprint of Thomas Nelson. W Publishing and Thomas Nelson are registered trademarks of HarperCollins Christian Publishing, Inc.

Published in association with Mary DeMuth Literary in Rockwall, Texas.

Thomas Nelson titles may be purchased in bulk for educational, business, fundraising, or sales promotional use. For information, please email SpecialMarkets@ThomasNelson.com.

ISBN 978-1-4003-4392-8 (audio)
ISBN 978-1-4003-4391-1 (ePub)
ISBN 978-1-4003-4390-4 (softcover)

Library of Congress Control Number: 2024947589

Printed in the United States of America

25 26 27 28 29 LBC 5 4 3 2 1

*To Aimée Powell, Allison Crumpton, Cheryl Clanahan,
Christie Moore, Connie Bradley, Holley Gerth, JulieAnne
Bruno, Kim Leonard, Maria Leonard, Rebecca Petersen,
Salena Duffy, Sherri Noah, and all the friends who've
been with me through the desperate and the delight. You're
a light in the dark reflecting the Light, and I love you.*

CONTENTS

Foreword   vii

A Short(ish) Introduction   xi

PART 1: HOW TO BE A GOOD FRIEND TO YOURSELF

1. Title Explained: Making a Sign to Hold in My Front Yard   3
2. It's Not Just You. Making Friends Is Hard.   13
3. Don't Discount the Fertilizer Seasons   23
4. Get Cozy and Comfortable with Awkward   33
5. Boundaries Are Your Friends   43
6. Boundaries Are Your Friends' Friends   55
7. Believe in Surprise Friendships   63
8. When Finding Friends Takes Forever, Ask Yourself
    These Questions   73

PART 2: HOW TO BE A GOOD FRIEND TO OTHERS

9. What You Can Expect Will Kill Your Friendships   85
10. Pioneer Up   95
11. Tell People What You Think of Them (No, Really)   105
12. *Freudenfreude* Is Your Relational Superpower   115
13. The Benefits of Bookend Friends   123
14. When a Friendship Ends Without Your Say-So   133

15. Rejection Sucks, but Don't Let It Suck You Down   143

16. Your Top-Notch Tool for Building Your Friendships   153

17. I Love My Friend to Pieces, but I Don't Love Her
    Views on _____   163

18. Leave Room for Mistakes   171

19. Making Friends by Showing Up   181

20. Making Friends by Opening Up   193

PART 3: WHAT A FRIEND WE HAVE IN JESUS

21. Making Friends by Praying Up   205

22. The Friend Who Never Fails in Friendship   215

Acknowledgments   225

Notes   229

About the Author   239

FOREWORD

I became friends with Kristen Strong on a good first impression, common interest, and a gut feeling.

We met online many years ago, back in the wild, wild west of blogging, where writers were giddy over meeting people who finally understood our unique ~~neurosis~~ relationship with words, while holding space for each other as we lamented our penchant for oversharing with strangers all over the world who now knew our preferred home remedies for constipation.

Kristen's warmth, even over the internet, immediately drew me in. She was genuinely kind—the type of person who repeats your name in a sentence—someone I would affectionately describe as "wouldn't hurt a fly."

We've been friends ever since.

I might have told you at one point in my life that internet friendships aren't real friendships. Only friends in "real life" count, where they have held your babies or know what your face looks like when you cry.

Those can certainly be rich friendships.

But so can internet friendships, I've found. Some of them, in fact, have become the dearest to me in recent years. They have developed into some of my most intimate friendships, supporting me through the death of my father, my children leaving for college, and a hysterectomy and entering menopause.

What makes for a real friendship isn't location. It is feeling safe, known, and loved by someone, even if they express most of it from afar. Kristen is one of those friends.

So when she told me she was writing a book on friendship, I got very excited. Not only is she the right person to write this book, but we all desperately need to read it as well.

In the same way I once judged the authenticity of internet friendships, I think we all tend to make many "friendship rules" for ourselves. What our friendships will look like, how they will come, who will be on the other side of them, and even how well we are doing inside of them by what we do or don't do—all of this becomes a cruel game with no winners.

We're so eager for "perfect" friendships, we wind up killing every friendship that threatens to grow with the looming fear that it won't.

In fact, I think it's why we struggle so much with friendships in general. We deeply want them, while we manage to dissect them to a slow death. (Does she really like me? Do we actually have things in common? Will I be good friend to her?)

We psych ourselves out of friendships before they even start, often based on failures of the past.

Take, for instance, how I used to judge myself for forgetting my friends' birthdays. "You don't really want to be my friend, trust me," I used to say to friend candidates from time to time, adding some laughs for good measure and then tacking on the reason: "I'll absolutely forget your birthday!"

It's not that I didn't want to be someone's friend. I just didn't want her to enter into a friendship with me under any false pretense. I felt I was saving us both the heartache of a potential friendship fracture from my fatal friendship flaw.

The truth is, I had friends in the past get upset with me for forgetting their birthdays. But I had taken their judgement upon myself now, too, believing my poor memory made me a crummy friend.

But one day I had a realization. I sat for an extended amount of time with a friend who was grieving and thought, *A good friend does that.* (I assure you, I am unfortunately quick to self-loathe, so I wasn't looking to give myself a pass or a compliment. I simply had a moment of revelation.)

We all have different strengths as people, so it makes sense that we also have different strengths as friends.

This is why Kristen's book is so important. We all need the same things—to get out of our heads, stop self-loathing and self-sabotaging, and be real about where we can and need to be better. No matter where we need to improve, we need real friends who love us for who we are. We need to not have to perform to be welcomed in. To know that just because we aren't great in one area doesn't mean we aren't a good friend. To stop killing friendships before they even start.

I love a lot of things about this wonderful book: Kristen's willingness to go first, tell the truth about friendship, and help us in this place where we all sometimes feel at a loss. I love her warmth. Her authenticity. Her kindness. All the things that drew me to her as a friend.

Maybe you make friends like I often do—you go off your gut. And maybe that's worked out for you, or maybe you've been burned in the process. Maybe you've had terrible luck with friends. Maybe you're afraid to try again, and on the outside you seem stone cold, but on the inside you're waving madly, *I'm over here! Please come sit with me!*

Or maybe, if you're honest, you've needed to be a better

friend, and it has nothing to do with forgetting someone's birthday. (PS: It's never too late to learn how to love people better.)

No matter where you are on your friendship journey, you've come to the right place. Kristen is the friend you need right now to help you open up, press on, heal, see something you haven't seen, and celebrate the beautiful, ever-surprising gift of friendship.

I am so happy to share my friend with you.

—Lisa Whittle,
BESTSELLING AUTHOR, SPEAKER,
AND PODCAST HOST

A SHORT(ISH) INTRODUCTION

Hello there, friend! And should you think I mean that in the watered-down, everyone-we-brush-virtual-elbows-with-on-social-media-is-a-friend kind of way, I don't. I may not know what town you call home or what your favorite color is, but I do know we both have a common, *desperate* interest in finding and keeping meaningful friendships. And because we share this goal, we're friends in that pursuit.

Whether you've read a bunch of fancy research on the subject or simply sense the changing environment we live in, know that it *is* harder to find friends today than it was in decades past. And no matter our age or season of life, we need friends.

I'm not exaggerating when I say that I wouldn't have made it through the past five years of my life without my friends. They saw me through some diff-i-cult days and seasons, staying with me—if not joining in—while I vented, raged, cried, and prayed. They listened well, made me laugh till I thought I'd split right open, and continually turned me in the direction of the Light.

We all need folks who do just that when life gets real lifey at us.

But I haven't always had a friend group like that. I haven't always known how to even be a friend. While I was never the "mean girl," I can tell you that from a young age I was the needy girl six ways from Sunday. I was a mess who didn't have a lick of interpersonal skills. Whether someone skews needy or mean, they allow insecurities to boss their behavior, just in different ways. When you're needy like I was, those insecurities cause you to tight-fist your friendships rather than hold them with a more relaxed posture. As a result, your friends, like a bird held too tightly, feel their stress levels rising. Naturally, this causes them to look for the quickest way to fly the coop altogether.

That is just one of several ways we can negatively influence our ability to be a good friend to others.

And while most—if not all—of us certainly know what it's like to be treated terribly by a "friend," we can also be a bad friend to ourselves.

When I was in eighth grade, I vividly remember going to a movie with my best friend, Haley. Not only was she as darling as the colorful Esprit sweatshirt she regularly sported, she was also wise beyond her tender thirteen years. At a time when I felt all knees and elbows in both appearance and confidence, Haley never left my presence without making me feel better about myself. In the sea of insincerity, insecurity, and false bravado that is middle school, Haley was a safe harbor of hype-girl encouragement and genuine friendship.

As those of us growing up in the eighties were wont to do, Haley and I often went to the movies together. On this particular night, as we settled into the plush seats two-thirds of the way back in the theater, we chatted about what Very Big Things were going on in our eighth-grade lives. Finally, *Crocodile Dundee II* began, and I happily opened my package of Twizzlers as I settled in to enjoy the show.

All was well until about halfway through the movie when a

growing uneasiness settled inside me. I looked at Haley as she munched popcorn. I looked around the dimly lit theater, but all appeared normal. That uneasiness in me grew and grew until the final credits rolled, and my stomach dropped as I heard a voice as dark as the theater whisper to me, *Haley doesn't really like you, Kristen. She just pretends to like you, and she's only here because she had nothing else to do. She doesn't like you cuz no one could ever really like you.*

As Haley and I stood to exit our row, I choked back a sob. I felt cold and wobbly, but I managed to swallow the threatening tears. At the same time, I was pretty practiced at putting on a brave front that in no way betrayed how I actually felt. Instead of letting Haley in on my fears in that moment, I fitted on that well-worn mask. After her mom dropped me off later that night and I retreated to the quiet of my bedroom, I cried like nobody's business.

What if all my friends merely tolerate me? In my thirteen-year-old mind I couldn't get past the fact it could be true.

In no way were my runaway thoughts founded in any kind of reality. And yet, whether we're thirteen, thirty, or sixty, we can convince ourselves that this kind of fiction *is* true.

I'm now middle-aged, and I still remember the dread I felt in that theater over the notion that those I thought were my friends, like Haley, may not have been my friends after all. What's more, that event planted a seed in me. Lies from childhood, like this one, can be like weeds taking root in the worst of environments. They find a way to grow in the dark without the encouragement of sunlight. And this particular lie would grow into a towering oak of insecurity that would take decades to uproot. Written across that oak was the word *unfriendable*. As a kid and as a grown-up, I've wondered if others merely tolerated me for my usefulness and functionality, like a lamp or a bedroom dresser.

> As a kid and as a grown-up, I've wondered if others merely tolerated me for my usefulness and functionality, like a lamp or a bedroom dresser.

Let's take a moment to pivot here and mention something that is very true of me: I am a woman of faith in the triune God: the Father; His Son, Jesus; and the Holy Spirit. If you do ascribe to a faith, I realize it may not reflect the same beliefs as my own. You're still most welcome as we journey through the pages in this book, because I want to help you with your friendships rather than get you to agree with me on every point I make. The Bible provides spiritual direction and solid hope for me and many others, so I do quote it frequently. It also provides practical help in many of life's struggles—including what it looks like to initiate and enjoy healthy friendships. The Bible is the needle of my life's compass that keeps me traveling in the right direction.

I won't shy away from this core belief of mine, but I've done my level best to make the language in this book friendly to all folks, whether you share my faith or not. Having said that, whether you agree with me or not, I want you to understand where I'm coming from.

In light of my faith, I can now see that episode in the movie theater for what it was: the Prince of Lies, aka the devil, trying to make me believe something that wasn't true. He forever seeks to isolate, kill, and destroy, and at that time I was an easier target than a rodent cornered by a rattlesnake. Thankfully, I've come to a place in my life where, while I'm not entirely bulletproof from the Enemy's poisonous ploys at bringing up old insecurities, I'm much more onto him.

Through a wealth of life experience that's seen me through every friendship circumstance under the sun, I've learned how to be a good friend to myself and to others so I can enjoy deep friendships *with* others. By the time you finish this book, I genuinely believe you'll know how to do the same.

Most of all, I want you to know that while friends may fail you, Jesus never will.

In his stellar book *The Four Loves*, C. S. Lewis wrote, "To the Ancients, Friendship seemed the happiest and most fully human of all loves; the crown of life and the school of virtue. The modern world, in comparison, ignores it."[1] He wrote that around 1960, quite a few decades ago, and as you can imagine, time has caused us to ignore its truth even more. Walls delineating property lines seem to get higher while our sense of isolation gets stronger. Writers of movies, television shows, and literature spill untold amounts of ink telling romantic stories. Considerably fewer stories are fashioned with friendship in mind—think *Steel Magnolias*, *A Different World*, and *Friends*.

Today's culture puts friendship on the back burner, but it needs to be placed front and center. Friendship is not a biological or sociological necessity, and yet it's of vital importance.[2] In the words of author Drew Hunter, "The wise person journeys through life neither alone nor in an impersonal crowd, but side by side with friends."[3]

Making friends is an extremely nuanced topic. Show me a checklist titled "Ten Rules for Making Friends," and I'll show you an exception to every rule listed. And yet, some general practices are very helpful in forming friendships. In the pages of this book, I've attempted to dial up the clarity on those practices as I've learned how to make and keep enduring friendships.

Sprinkled with sass and saturated in real talk with a side of Okie vernacular, *Desperate Woman Seeks Friends* will help you know you're not alone in your friendship struggles. It'll show you how to push through rejection till you find connection again. And it'll see you to your own side-by-side friendships.

One note about the text itself: Some names used in this book have been changed. I don't want anyone who may've been a bad friend at one point in my life to feel shame for how they treated me if they come across this book. It's always possible that someone can become a better friend today than they were yesterday. I know that as well as anyone.

You may be desperate for friends, like I've been, but I'm curious if, out of your own desperation, you've ever considered doing something I considered doing one evening in 2005. Turn the page to read more.

PART 1

HOW TO BE A GOOD FRIEND TO YOURSELF

Simple principles and practices to help you stay grounded with a healthy mindset so you bring your best self to others—and don't inadvertently sabotage your efforts to make friends.

CHAPTER 1

TITLE EXPLAINED:
MAKING A SIGN TO HOLD
IN MY FRONT YARD

Desperation is a necessary ingredient
to learning anything or creating
anything. Period. If you ain't desperate
at some point, you ain't interesting.
JIM CARREY

n 2004, our family moved from an active, treasured community to a new neighborhood in a new state. With two freshly
minted five-year-olds and a one-year-old, as well as a husband who worked long, crazy hours as a member of the United
States Air Force, I spent significantly more time starved for adult
conversation than satisfied from it. I missed my friends terribly,

but I figured I'd make new local ones. All I had to do was roll up my sleeves and put in the work required to place myself in the proximity of others. After all, I had small kids, which meant that I would regularly cross paths with other moms of small kids at any number of places. Or perhaps I'd gel with some of the women who attended our church. My husband, David, worked with some great guys and gals who, along with their spouses or significant others, could double-date with us. The possibilities of friends from our pools of people that we regularly came in contact with were endless!

How long could this take? I thought to myself, chock-full of hope and positivity.

Not long, I assumed.

Yeah, I assumed wrong.

I extended invitation after invitation, only to be met with lackluster responses. Everyone around me seemed to already have their people, and they had no time in their schedules or interest in their lives for more people.

One evening, while I was especially sad and missing close-by gal pals somethin' fierce, an idea popped into my head. When my husband returned home later that evening, I shared this bit of brilliance with him. In an effort to find friends, I would make a sign that read "Desperate Woman Seeks Friends!" and hold it at the corner of our front yard by the street.

My husband stared at me wide-eyed.

"Are you really going to do that?" he said, tilting his head sideways.

"I just might!" I responded, drumming my fingertips on my chin in contemplation.

If this had occurred today, I could've created a social media post with a picture of me holding this Desperate Woman Seeks Friends! sign. But since this occurred in ye olden days before social media, holding a sign in my front yard would've been the old-timey way of accomplishing the same thing. I'm a doer by nature, and I certainly didn't consider myself above an action like this, one that might provide a solution to my problem if a nice, lonely-for-friends gal happened to see it.

To be truthful, I was every bit of desperate to find another woman with whom I could talk and laugh and share troubles with in person. Yet even my doer self couldn't find one.

The most frustrating part? I was willing to put effort into initiating friendships. I would walk over to others and introduce myself. I asked others questions about themselves. I suggested outings. I invited people over. And while a few interactions led to a second conversation or get-together, most stalled out, not enough altitude gained to be able to catch a breeze and soar toward anything meaningful.

While that period of my life stands out as the longest I've gone without local friends, it was hardly the first time I struggled to find my people.

In my mind's eye, I can still see my tired, twentysomething self, out of breath from hurrying (though I'm still late) and forcing my stubborn side-by-side double stroller up the hill to the playgroup location, an indoor playground. I'm nervous too, since I'm visiting for the first time. I heave the heavy door open and awkwardly bang the double stroller against the frame half a dozen times before making it through. (Thank God He gave babies the ability to take a little jostling, because heaven knows how often I jostled my twins while maneuvering their Buick-sized stroller through a heavy door.) Once inside and settled, I approach moms and chat as best I can while wrangling wiggly toddlers. However, it doesn't take long to figure out that this familiar, established mom sorority isn't interested in pursuing conversation with me beyond introductions.

A short while later, after another move to a different state, I find another local moms' group. Soon after joining, I volunteer to host a meeting in my home. I clean, cook snacks, and wrestle kids into fresh clothes. Then I wait and wait as not one single soul shows up at my house.

Then there was that time more recently when a gal with whom I thought I was building a friendship with suddenly stopped responding to my texts and messages. After staring at my phone for the umpteenth time, willing a response from her to appear, I looked up and out the window as my mind formed a sudden realization.

Ohhh. So this is what being ghosted looks and feels like.

That wasn't the first time someone had changed their mind about being my friend, but it was the first time I'd put that language to it.

In an effort to find friends, I've swung the bat and missed the ball. *A lot.* I've faced rejection a lot. So what's a girl to do when she's plumb tuckered from trying to make friends but knows she still needs them?

She keeps trying.

Because the only surefire way to know you'll never make friends is to never try to make friends.

While I've swung and missed quite a bit, I've hit some home runs too. If I had let the fear of striking out convince me never to step up to the plate again, I wouldn't have one single thriving friendship today. Having said that, I know as well as anyone that women can wound us, convincing us they're not worth the effort.

If I'm speaking on the topic of friendship to a group of women, I will often comment during my talk that women can be . . . tricky. Every time I mention that, without fail, I watch the collective group of heads nodding up and down in agreement. When it comes to making friendships, some of us are just plain scared to try again because it feels a little like going into battle without our protective armor. Entertaining the thought of a friendship is too vulnerable, too scary, and it leaves our hearts and heads too exposed. We've collected enough of our own war stories involving women through the years, thank ya kindly, and we don't need to add more to our personal compendiums.

In the United States, Americans have fewer close friends than they did thirty years ago.[1] And while more recent events—namely a global pandemic—can be partially blamed for the overall decline in friendships, wider cultural shifts may have contributed to the issue at hand. We live in a world where so many in-person friendships are replaced by the diluted online kind. Our increased involvement with social media is temporarily scratching the itch of finding friends, but unless we're growing those friendships we first make online into real, face-to-face ones, they're unlikely to become the deep, fulfilling relationships we desire.

Liking a social media post alone doesn't make one a friend. Loving a person through the gifts of our own presence and prayers (and perhaps a caffeinated beverage or two) makes one a friend.

Another cultural change is that Americans are more geographically mobile than ever before, so more folks must reinvent their local friendship landscape more than ever before. Also, today's parents spend twice as much time with their children than parents of past generations.[2] So if a parent's available time on any given day is represented by a pie, there's a slimmer slice to be enjoyed with friends.

Whatever our life stages and life experiences, it's getting harder to make friends, not easier. Yet we all need them because as we age, "friendship is one of the key factors in finding . . . happiness."[3] And we are happiest when we have a couple of real friends—those we're around not because of our utility to one another or familial obligation. Of course, this isn't to say we can't be good friends with family! For example, I consider my sister-in-law, Lisa, a great friend, as well as other family members. But beyond being family, we connect over shared interests and life circumstances. We're together because we enjoy each other, and each of us needs real friends for the same reason.[4] We need real friends because research shows that deeper conversations—not simply small talk—make people happier, and "self-disclosure" brings closeness in relationships.[5]

Those are the kindergarten components of meaningful friendship.

While I'm much more interested in *your* personal story that brought you to this book rather than sweeping statistics, it's still true that research conducted with large groups of people is useful in that it shows us we aren't alone in feeling lonely. We aren't alone in our desire to make friends, just like we're not alone in our desire to get through a painful friendship breakup. Also, we're not alone in the negative consequences that come from a lack of friends. Several years ago, a study revealed that while life expectancy has improved in many places worldwide, it's declining in the United States. This is the first time that's happened since World War I.[6]

Our extreme loneliness is contributing to this decreased life expectancy, which is causing the same rate of loss for Americans as a *world war.* If that ain't a sobering thought, I don't know what is.

Whether we like it or not, whether we think we can get by without friends or not, smart scientific people have proved what many of our hearts already know: We need real-deal friendships.

While my nearly twenty years as a military wife gave me a lot of tried-and-true education on how to make friends (as well as the awkwardness, adversity, and, yes, fertilizer involved), the ten-plus years since David's retirement from the military—and our subsequent staying in the same city for that entire time—have shown me how hard it can be to make friends even when you've lived in the same place for a long time.

I've been the new girl and the been-around-a-while girl, and I've learned that each has its advantages and disadvantages. Yet, it's equally possible for both kinds of people to make friends—the lifelong kind that stick by you through the roller-coaster rides and calm, beachy times of life.

But if we want that reward, we need to get comfortable with an uncomfortable truth: Friendships, like all marital and familial relationships, require work. So where do we direct those efforts?

That is where I aim to be of service to you through this book. No matter what you've been through in your attempts to befriend or be friended by other women, chances are there's a story, or ten, in this book that reflect a bit of your own story, one that will help you try again to find the friends you need. That's what my heart wants to give you through these pages: hope and direction to try again—as well as reassurance to keep on keepin' on when that task is ridiculously hard due to rejection or just plain mean behavior someone else threw your way. (Hello, let's stop thinking that mean girls cease to exist after high school!)

I want to help you first be a good friend to yourself by learning principles and practices to stay grounded and healthy so you bring your best self to others. And I want to help you be a good friend to others by sharing principles and practices to help you grow and deepen your friendships with others. They'll give life to your friendships so you don't inadvertently strangle the life right out of them. Finally, I want you to know that Jesus knows what it's like to be hurt and betrayed by friends. Yet, He's the only life-saving Friend who'll never let you down.

I hope to be your walk-alongside companion in your quest to find good friends, the true-blue kind who excel at the old-fashioned art of listening with eye contact and knowing when you need a hug, a latte, or a little righteous indignation on your behalf. The kind who know when your birthday is and don't hesitate to tell you how cute you look in your jeans. The kind who know when something's wrong, because you don't have the energy or desire to be around them and pretend that it's not. The kind you can call at 2:00 a.m. to watch your kid because you have to take her older brother to the emergency room, and your spouse is out of town. The kind who ask, "What can I do?" and then do what you need. Or the one who doesn't ask, because she's already doing it—making the soup, picking up the kids, and telling you things are or aren't as bad as they appear. You deserve the kind of friend you can trust to talk kindly about you when you're standing next to her, as well as when you're not.

I'm a flawed person and far from a perfect pal, and if you think otherwise, stick with me these next several pages and I'll slam shut that notion real quick-like. Still, I've learned a good deal about how to persevere through the often-discouraging-yet-still-worth-it world of getting friendship wrong, missing connections, bringing the extra-awkward, making a mess of relationships, and, by the grace of the good Lord above, getting it imperfectly right in a way that has led to lasting, meaningful friendships.

Is it easier said than done? Yep. But is it absolutely doable? Oh yes. Jesus, who was perfect in all ways, had friends. He had His twelve apostles, and within that circle He had his closest friends, Peter, James, and John (Matthew 10:2–3; Mark 5:37). Of course, He had other friends whom He crossed paths with during His ministry, such as Lazarus, Mary, Martha, and Mary Magdalene.

If Jesus walked this planet with friends, you and I need to do the same. And it's God's heart for all of us to have our people. You are not the exception to that.

One more time for the person in the back: *You are not the exception to that.*

If you're a college student trying to find your people on a sprawling campus or in a home that isn't the one you grew up in, you are not the exception to that.

If you're a twenty- or thirtysomething needing help connecting with people who speak in full sentences (aka not your tiny children), you are not the exception to that.

If you're a fortysomething trying to find a real friend in your fast-paced work environment, you are not the exception to that.

If you're a fiftysomething who realizes you've spent years encouraging your kids' friendships and yet are sorely lacking in your own, you are not the exception to that.

If you're a sixty- or seventy-year-old in the stage of life when your kids are busy with their own lives and you need to widen your circle, you are not the exception to that.

And if you're eighty or older and just want to know how to use your years of immense, hard-fought wisdom to be a welcoming place for others, you are not the exception to that.

This book is for you. No matter your age or life stage, this book is for anyone who's discouraged in her pursuit of friendpeople and needs to know the process is hard because it *is* hard, not because there's anything wrong with her.

I never did make that sign and stand in my yard with it, although I was *thiiiis* close. After all, I had the posterboard and markers *and* a deep supply of desperation. As it turned out, right after that time, I met my friend Sherri because we both kept showing up at our neighborhood park at the same time with our young children. Sherri and I haven't lived in the same town since 2007, but we're still friends today.

You never know how or when God may orchestrate a change in circumstances for the better.

I have no clue how to do helpful things like change a tire or tile my bathroom floor, but I do know what helps us do the significant work of finding and making friends. Good friends. And if you'll allow me the privilege, I'll offer you the opportunity to learn the same in a safe, non-desperate-y way.

Your real-life assignment beyond sticking with me through these pages?

Don't give up. Don't close off your heart.

Do keep trying.

HOW TO BE A GOOD FRIEND TO YOURSELF

If Jesus walked this planet with people, He wants you to as well, because it's the Father's heart for you to have friends. You're not the exception. Be a good friend to yourself by keeping a try-again mindset in your pursuit to find your people.

CHAPTER 2

IT'S NOT JUST YOU. MAKING FRIENDS IS HARD.

You can't stay in your corner of the
Forest waiting for others to come to you.
You have to go to them sometimes.
A. A. MILNE

In chapter 1, I shared my frustration over putting in the work to build friendships, only to be met with yawning responses. While this is true, it's also true that I wasn't always willing to put in the time and work to initiate friendships with others. What's more, I didn't have a clue about how one goes out and (waves hand ambiguously in the air) "makes friends."

I grew up on what I still consider a most beautiful plot of land: O'Neill Lane in Osage County, Oklahoma. O'Neill was my last name and the last name of everyone living on that lane. The lane's name reflected the lane's environment: a firm foundation of family and security that was as sturdy and strong as the many towering oak trees that populated it. More than I could ever understand while growing up, I benefited from the sheltering shade and the deep, expansive root system of my own family tree.

With that root system came a captivating cocoon of familiarity in fun, feisty family members. For many of my growing-up years, I had a network of friends who only helped to water and feed my sense of belonging. We sat side by side in classes together from middle school through high school, and some of them traipsed forty-two miles down the road to the same college where I went—as did my sisters and several other members of my family.

Even in college, my family and friends were simply always there.

While attending Oklahoma State University (Go Pokes!), I fell in love with a tall, dark, and handsome fellow with the most dazzling chocolate-brown eyes I'd ever seen. His work ethic and easygoing confidence didn't hurt my attraction toward him either.

Neither did the way his muscly arms filled out the sleeves of his T-shirt.

Sigh.

While at Oklahoma State, David was also going through the ROTC program to commission into the United States Air Force. So when he got down on one knee and held up a diamond ring that I exuberantly accepted, I knew that meant I would be joining him in the military life. I knew that meant we'd move wherever the USAF told us to move. But I didn't give much thought to the fact that it also meant I would have to develop a brand-new community again and again.

I hadn't a clue as to how difficult and discouraging that endeavor would so often be.

Two weeks after we married in my hometown church surrounded by the jackpot of family and friends, we moved to Ohio, where I knew not one solitary soul. For me, whose family and friends had always been around, Ohio might as well have been the moon for how different it looked and felt. Add to that the fact that the one person I did know, my beloved husband, traveled all the everlovin' time, and I had myself an equation for severe loneliness.

Having recently celebrated my fiftieth birthday, I still look back on that time as one of the loneliest of my life. Not once have I regretted marrying the good man I did. Yet, getting myself used to a new state, a new university, and a new marriage took so much more out of me than my idealistic twentysomething self could've imagined.

Thinking back to my newlywed years, I give myself so much more grace now because *of course it was hard*. Being a newbie at something—let alone several new things at once—almost always means we're not too good at the thing(s) we're just now becoming acquainted with or learning about. And finding community is certainly no different. While some people are wired with a natural ability to excel at making friends, it's still a learned art and skill.

And in those early days and months and years of my marriage, I didn't have one iota of that art or skill.

What I did have was a husband who was gone more than he was home and a homesickness that ate me from the inside out. One would think this reality would've forced me to reach out to others over and over, but alas, it did not.

While I did try to reach out to a small number of folks at the college I had transferred to, my new marital status, as well as the fact that I commuted to college (and talked with an accent as thick as molasses), made it hard to connect with students there. I would tentatively dip my toe into the ocean of vulnerability required when meeting someone new and just as quickly yank it out when my overture was met with what felt like a shark bite of rejection. Cue me hightailing it to safer territory, certain this whole finding-friends thing wasn't worth the pain.

Now, I realize that is a dramatic response to a failed connection—or in my case, connections. But again, I was new at putting myself out there to meet others, so it didn't take much resistance for me to quit.

Discouraged that my minimal efforts brought a lot of failure, I reasoned that since God surely wanted me to have friends, He would bring them my way. Therefore, I was officially off the hook from doing anything else to actively pursue friendships myself.

So in those early days of trying to find friends yet possessing little ability to persevere through the process, I remained perpetually frustrated that no one would reach out and try to make friends with me. My own loneliness and propensity to feel sorry for myself pushed me to withdraw further and further inward.

This led me to develop the biggest victim mentality east of the Mississippi, which caused me to cough up excuse after excuse for why I couldn't make a connection with anyone.

I can't find friends here because the people aren't as friendly.
I can't find friends here because of the long winters, when everyone stays inside.
I can't find friends here because people already have their people.

I can't find friends here because no one asks me questions about myself.

I can't find friends here because there's something wrong with me.

And listen, some of these statements were absolutely true. For example, when you transfer from one school to another as a college senior, most people *do* already have their people. But I let those excuses be the beginning and end of the matter, and I swallowed the belief that I was a victim set up for failure. I crossed my arms and told myself, *Just accept this now, Kristen. You're not going to have friends till you graduate and move again.*

Having said that, when trying to make friends, sometimes it's true that the odds for success *are* stacked against you. When I transferred colleges from Oklahoma State to one in Ohio, at least one person flat-out told me my accent made me sound dumb. Most of the people I went to school with were ridiculously wealthy, especially for college students. A friend who was a music education major like me grew up with David Letterman as her neighbor. My neighbors growing up—other than a smattering of family members—were Holstein dairy cows. Between that and the fact that my marital status and school commute kept me on the fringes of campus life, it's easy to see how the odds of finding my people were stacked against me.

While this was all true, it hardly made me a victim. First of all, regardless of what we see in someone else's life, everyone deals with rough friendship patches to one degree or another. I certainly wasn't the first. Some folks suffer painful rejection from a friend they've known for decades, not just from new people. Second, while I was in circumstances that made finding friends more difficult, it wasn't impossible. It was a bigger hill for me to climb, yes, but that just meant I needed to put in the work and be willing to sweat some more before I successfully crested the peak of that hill.

And while new things rarely come easily to us, that doesn't mean more practice at the activity will suddenly mean it's forever and always easier afterward. It might, of course. The more I practiced musical instruments in my growing-up years, the more proficient I became at them. Yet, even when I played in a professional group, an exceptionally hard piece could throw me for a loop. Could I eventually master it? Absolutely. But the reality of a harder piece of music means I'll have to put in the work by practicing all the more to get the notes in my head and under my fingers.

And so it goes with friendship. New realities and difficult changes to the friendship landscape simply mean I'll need to get comfortable with practicing more at finding my people.

With a fresh awareness of that truth back in Ohio in 1996, as well as a newly discovered determination not to let loneliness get the last word, I decided I needed to risk rejection and try finding friends again. An oboist in a quintet, I invited the other four members of my ensemble to my apartment for a little party. To my delighted surprise, they all accepted my invitation. So I put together my mom's cheese-and-olive dip with crackers and a sheet cake from a box mix. I cobbled together a punch made primarily of ice cream and Sprite like we were meeting for a reception in a church basement. On a chilly February night, two-thirds of the way through the school year, my guests walked through my front door. We talked and laughed and cleaned up the vittles as only college kids can do.

I would love to tell you that after that little party, the five of us became best buddies who still regularly live it up together. We do not. I haven't talked to any of them in decades. *But* that wobbly invitation I extended did two important things for my outlook on finding friends:

1. It broke the ice by helping me feel more comfortable with those folks, and it helped them get to know me beyond quick conversations before and after rehearsals.
2. It taught me I can be brave and open up my home to other people in spite of not knowing them very well.

If I'd continued to allow my hurt feelings from rejection boss me around and keep me from extending an invitation for that night in 1996, I would've missed a genuinely fun evening in the short term. But in the long term, I would've missed out on learning that rejection doesn't have to be the end of the story. Would that lesson have been imparted to me later on? I think so. But I'm so thankful I learned it when I did.

That year taught me so much about how to accept my circumstances rather than react to them, to keep trying again instead of allowing rejection to coerce me into a victim mentality. That is easier to do if you don't let the devil persuade you that you're the only one going through friendship foibles. Author Sally Clarkson writes, "One of the worst things the enemy can do is to convince us that our situation is unique, that we are completely alone, and that we will never be able to make it out to see situations resolved. While it's easy to believe that we are unique in these times of darkness [and] difficulty, scripture is filled with stories of disaster and destruction."[1]

Sally goes on to mention how, when things looked rather bleak for Paul and the others tossed around on a ship during a nor'easter-type storm on the Adriatic Sea, he chose to encourage his shipmates. In Acts 27, Paul said, "But now I urge you to keep up your courage, because not one of you will be lost; only the ship will be destroyed. Last night an angel of the God to whom I belong and whom I serve stood beside me and said, 'Do not be afraid, Paul'" (vv. 22–24).

Paul encouraged them to stay the course because the Lord would see them through that trial. And while finding friends isn't a trial like facing the possibility of death in a shipwreck, it can be a long, nausea-inducing journey that inspires one to consider giving up altogether.

Yet I urge you to keep up your courage.

God wants you to have your friends—it's His will for you.

About four years ago, my supersmart business coach, Retha, mentioned that when it comes to something work-related, I tend to think I'm the only one going through it. When she said that, I immediately thought, *Daggum, Kristen . . . look at you sporting that blasted victim mentality with parts of your work.*

What I'm saying is, while I long ago dropped the victim mentality with my friendships and generally have a handle on that, I haven't overcome it elsewhere! So please know I'm not casting stones at you for wherever it shows up. But I am saying it's time for you and me to give any propensity for it an honest evaluation so we can deal with it. Considering the Enneagram personality model, I'm a strong Two whose heart gushes empathy like a fire hose, so I understand the real and present struggles with the real and present pain that you've experienced in the past. Heck, I've felt it myself and sometimes still do. But we must look at things as they are so we can move forward to where we want to be. *Finding friends is hard because it's hard to find friends.* It's hard because these things take time. Let's be a friend to ourselves by resisting the urge to sabotage our efforts with a victim mentality.

Let's be friends to ourselves by not expecting everyone else to do the work. Friends don't appear out of nowhere á la Harry Potter, as nice as it would be if they did. Wouldn't it be great if we could saunter into a coffee shop and find our Monica, Rachel, and Phoebe? Yet, real life isn't a sitcom where we simply wait for friends to magically show up. Instead, we get out and about in an effort to cross paths with folks, in an effort to get to know folks.

You aren't unfriendable—or rather you're not destined to be friendless. You're just becoming more closely acquainted with the fact that this business of finding friends is hard. The only thing that makes you unfriendable is never putting yourself out there again, and we need you too much for that nonsense.

Lysa TerKeurst writes, "It's impossible to hold up the banners of victim and victory at the same time."[2]

Victim may have been a chapter or three in your story in trying to find your people, but it doesn't have to be the final chapter. It doesn't have to define the narrative.

Keep at it, and victory will be yours.

I'm cheering you on all along the way.

HOW TO BE A GOOD FRIEND TO YOURSELF

Each of us endures friendship struggles. Think about what it would mean to be a victor through your friendship difficulties rather than a victim of them. Rejection doesn't have to be the end of your story. Be a good friend to yourself by pushing past the hard and extending an invite to just one person in your circle. You never know where one invitation could lead!

CHAPTER 3

DON'T DISCOUNT THE FERTILIZER SEASONS

*I have taken all of the manure that has been
thrown at me all my life and used it as fertilizer.*
EARTHA KITT

I f I may be rather blunt, the friendship situation surrounding my daughter's high school years was a bunch of crap.

Technically, she did have friends in high school. But for most of her time there, they were akin to our weather here in Colorado: fluctuating and wildly inconsistent.

When Faith entered her freshman year, she felt relieved to be starting at the same high school as a smattering of friends from her middle school. As familiarity breeds comfort, she thought this group of gal pals would make her transition to high school easier. Yet, the first couple of weeks revealed that these girls would make the transition harder, not easier. One moment, they would be warm and engaging. The next, they were cold and distant. And when those stretches of unfriendliness would naturally force Faith to invest her time in other people, these same girls would seek her out and accuse her of behaving like a snob who thought she was too good for them.

The maddening cycle continued till the summer after junior year when one of the girls appeared to have a marked change in conscience. She gave Faith a heartfelt apology for her past ugliness and told her that she would do better. Faith, not one to naturally assume she is without fault in conflict, apologized for anything she had done to contribute to their rocky relationship. Following that conversation, Faith's heart illuminated from the inside out, and she glowed with the certainty that a whole tree's worth of new leaves had been turned over for a beautifully fresh start just in time for senior year.

That miraculous change lasted a month, maybe two. And then the cruel, hot-and-cold, up-and-down cycle began all over again.

I can still see Faith's crestfallen face as she told me, "Mom, I'm done. I gave it my best, but I won't make the mistake of trusting these girls again—or talking with them again."

I hugged her and told her that indeed this was a testimony to the adage, "When people show you who they are, believe them." I told her that true to her character, she had given them the benefit of the doubt over and over, and now it was time to be a good friend to herself by cutting ties with these girls.

For the majority of Faith's senior year, she and the girls barely spoke to one another, and Faith was the better for it.

During this time, other "friends" displayed troubling behaviors as well. For example, Faith would invite a classmate or two to meet for coffee, see a movie together, or visit our house to bake something or see our assemblage of animals. And while she did get together with friends from time to time, a frustrating number of them would excitedly accept her invitation only to later cancel with a vague, lame excuse right before their scheduled meeting time. Over and over, I witnessed my daughter plunge from the "heights of happiness" to the depths of despair (borrowing a phrase from my favorite literary heroine, Anne Shirley) following these abrupt changes in plans. The continual lack of basic social graces I witnessed discouraged and frustrated Faith to no end.

Their behavior made me see red as her mama.

Thankfully, Faith formed genuine friendships through her tennis-club team, and that helped fill some of the gaps in her community of peers. And while Faith did find a couple of kind friends in high school, those years were largely lonely for her because she never found a deep sense of belonging. The pandemic, which affected her sophomore and junior years, certainly didn't help her ability to find her people at school.

When the time came for Faith to head to college at Texas A&M, she was positively giddy to begin this next stage of her life. While she often repeated how much she would miss her family and pets, she was very excited to see what friend potential college held for her.

And oh my stars, what potential it held and positive outcomes it delivered. From the moment she hit the sacred grounds of College Station, Faith made friends with folks wherever she went. She made a friend in her roommate, friends in her major, friends in club tennis, friends in the dining hall, and friends in campus ministry group and volunteer organizations. The girl made friends left, right, and center. While her dad and I missed her somethin' fierce (and still do!), we practically jumped up and down to see our girl come fully alive with delight and contentment as she made a solid place for herself in college.

Now, I'm not naive, and I know that friend problems crop up for her there the same as anywhere else, no matter how ideal the locational setup. But it has done Faith a world of good to put in the work to make friends and have that effort rewarded with a harvest of friendships.

While Faith was home on Christmas break following her first semester at A&M, her dad and I sat with her in our living room discussing the drastic change experienced between the high school years and those first months in college. Reflecting on both periods of time, I said, "Darlin' child, on the friend front, your high school years were full of crap. At A&M, you're reaping the rewards of a harvest well earned."

And then my husband quipped, "Harvests do better with a lot of fertilizer, and you've stored up some fertilizer that you're now putting to good use."

I haven't forgotten that statement, because it's true: In God's economy, nothing is waste or wasted. And in the natural world, a good deal of fertilizer helps good things grow.

In not-too-poetic terms, gross stuff helps grow essential stuff.

Fertilizers, which often contain manure, provide the nutrients plants need to thrive. Plants require an enormous amount of energy to grow a strong root system, sprout leaves, and produce food. Fertilizer helps plants succeed at all these things.[1]

While manure commonly used for gardening (largely of the horse, cow, or chicken variety) is packed with beneficial nutrients like nitrogen and phosphorus for plants, it's often mixed with compost to ensure it doesn't burn or hurt the plants underneath. But if the manure is well aged, it doesn't contain excess amounts of nutrients that could harm plants.[2] Therefore, it can be applied to the soil all on its own.[3] Well-aged manure offers other benefits, such as boosting a plant's natural immunity, preventing weeds, and improving soil structure, since it acts as a slow-release fertilizer that doesn't wash out of the soil quickly.

Another big bonus of well-aged manure as fertilizer? It doesn't smell.

Why am I going on and on about manure, especially the well-aged variety? Because I want you to see that, like well-aged fertilizer, your long, well-aged trials can still lead to an abundant harvest. This certainly applies to the friendship front. If you've experienced your own years of accumulating fertilizer, take heart: Your harvest will come eventually. Yesterday's hardships from trying to make friends feed our present-day and future friendships.

Through her high school years, my daughter learned a great deal about what a good friend does and doesn't do. She learned what friendship qualities she valued. She examined her own heart and attitude to see what behaviors needed to be left behind, as well as what lies about her worth needed to be thrown out. Having known all too well what it was to be on the outside, she learned

> Yesterday's hardships from trying to make friends feed our present-day and future friendships.

the skill of reaching out to others in hopes of establishing a connection—to bring them in. She learned there are different kinds of friendships and how to know when a friendship is and isn't meant to be.

Faith discovered that learning to deal with rejection is its own gift because it's an important life skill. She learned that rejection, while terribly difficult, isn't the end of the world.

Her fertilizer experiences were beneficial by way of lessons learned, and that fertilizer continues to grow a bumper crop of friendships for her today.

My daughter's high school experiences highlighted some

fundamental truths of what does make a good friend. And while we can chalk up some of the behaviors Faith encountered to young girls still learning social graces, I've talked with many a grown-up woman whose own experiences reflect some of my daughter's. We'll talk about some of these in more detail later on, but for now, here are a few good friendship habits we'll want to develop so we can set ourselves up to be the kind of friend each one of us would like to have:

1. **LET YOUR YES BE YES AND YOUR NO BE NO.** Matthew 5:37 tells us, "Let your 'Yes' be 'Yes,' and your 'No,' 'No.' For whatever is more than these is from the evil one" (NKJV). If we say yes to an invitation extended by a friend, then for the love of all that's holy, let's follow through on that commitment. Of course, the reality of life means that a knot in our schedules can cause plans to change. Days with unforeseen disruptions call for flexibility. But changing plans at the last minute when (we perceive) a better option has become available to us is selfish and unkind.

2. **EXERCISE VULNERABILITY AND RECIPROCITY.** Trying again for the good friends you need requires your heart to be turned inside out from time to time as you judiciously but vulnerably share with someone how you're really doing. But it also means giving the other person the space to do the same. It's not kind or fair to monopolize the conversation by talking only about yourself, or to repeatedly redirect the conversation back to yourself.

   Of course, from time to time, you may get together with someone who gets more of the floor because she's going through a particularly difficult time and needs to share and process. You will likely need to do the same at times. But no one should be the only one doing it all the time. In general, though, learning to ask questions of each other and actually listening to the answers goes a long way toward fostering a life-giving friendship for both parties. And just as it's not ideal for one person to monopolize the conversation by talking only about herself, it's also unfair for one person to insist on vulnerability from the other person while withholding it herself.

Case in point: I have a dear friend who is a fantastic listener to my struggles, but she is very reticent to share her own. *Ever.* Now, if our relationship were more mentor-mentee, this could fly. But it's not. So it can be awkward to share with her because it starts to feel like she's just interested in my drama to either make her feel better about her own or to maintain a front that she doesn't have any struggles (which we *all* do). Perhaps this isn't her motive at all, but because I end up doing most of the talking—no matter how often I redirect things back to her—it still comes across as a sort of one-sided friendship. So I'm less inclined to share. It's best when, over the course of time, *both* parties regularly share their struggles, causing them to experience the benefits of feeling seen, validated, and known through mutual encouragement.

3. **DON'T PRESENT YOURSELF AS THE HERO OR THE VICTIM OF EVERY STORY.** Recently, a fellow writer friend of mine, Chelsea, told me that after sharing a parenting struggle she had regarding one of her children, her friend shrugged and said with an air of bewilderment, "Huh. I just can't relate to that!" Then, as this friend frequently does, she proceeded to detail an amazing reward her kid had received. This is problematic not because the friend couldn't identify with that particular parenting struggle. The problem was in how she chose to respond,

setting herself and her kid up as heroes. Not only did her response seriously discourage Chelsea, but Chelsea quickly learned not to share parenting struggles with this friend anymore. This means she no longer connects with that friend like she thought she could.

If we, in humility, listen with empathy, regardless of whether we identify with the expressed problem or not, we build the bonds of connection and therefore open the door so the other person can share how she's really doing. Besides, the only hero in any success story is the good Lord above, whose gift of grace shows up in us humans. Remembering this will help us to be the kind of friends we want to have.

Likewise, we don't want to present ourselves as the victim of every story. That's not because we don't want to share our struggles with others, including the hard times that have befallen us. But if you find yourself regularly giving in to a spirit of victimhood, it's a short bridge from that to behaviors such as monopolizing conversations and one-upmanship. By all means, share what you've been through; it's validating to hear a friend say, "I'm so sorry that happened to you." But be mindful that your motive behind it is to share vulnerably, not to wallow in self-pity.

4. **BE A FAITHFUL FRIEND.** Faithfulness is a quality in friendships that's falling by the wayside, which is sad because it's as important as it ever was to be a faithful friend. Yes, friendships either grow or dwindle. But as you examine the friendships in your life, they shouldn't all be dwindling—at least as far as you can control. There should be a small number of friends you feel compelled to stick with for the long haul. Even if your relationship with someone changes and you're not as similar as you

used to be, you can still be a faithful friend who sees and names the good that shouts as a beautiful testimony of her life. You can certainly still commit to being there for the other person and letting every interaction with them be fed by that truth. Now, I'm all for pursuing a new friendship as the Lord places a particular person in your path and on your heart. But if you find yourself constantly doing this at the expense of other healthy friendships, perhaps you need to ask yourself if you're falling for a "grass is greener" way of thinking.

With these good habits under our hats, we can move forward in confidence that we are setting ourselves up for success on the friend front, even if we don't feel like we have the harvest of friendships around us (yet!) to prove it. Harvests take time to grow, and your time will come.

Recently, I came across this passage of Scripture in which Paul told the Ephesians, "I keep asking that the God of our Lord Jesus Christ, the glorious Father, may give you the Spirit of wisdom in revelation, so that you may know him better" (Ephesians 1:17).

As you endure your own season of accumulating well-aged fertilizer, I pray God gives you His Spirit of wisdom in revelation regarding your own friendship harvest. And as you and I work to refine our own quirks and behaviors so they don't contribute to other people's fertilizer, I pray He gives us wisdom in revelation that helps us grow in social graces that bless rather than blight others. As with each of us, God is renewing your strength and vision day by day, season by season. He is not idle but is actively moving in your life *so that you may know Him better*. Part of that is showing you and me how hardships that seemed so unnecessary before can grow into future blessings rising from the mystery.

One of my favorite authors, Bonnie Gray, sent an email to me that included the following line: "God is amazing—Jesus uses EVERY moment in our lives to weave us into wholeness [so we may] then share what we've learned to walk alongside other women."[4]

I love this because it succinctly describes why God doesn't waste one drop of our difficulties. Every moment of every struggle will be straightened and stitched into a beautiful tapestry of wholeness. Then we can take what we've learned and walk alongside other women in their own friendship struggles.

Before long, we'll see that what felt and looked like waste was not wasted in God's hands.

HOW TO BE A GOOD FRIEND TO YOURSELF

Think of the lessons learned during your own fertilizer season. Be a good friend to yourself and accept that these lessons, though terribly difficult to endure, are gifts that will feed your future friendships. While fertilizer seasons stink to high heaven, stick with it and rest assured your most well-aged trials *will* lead to an abundant harvest.

CHAPTER 4

GET COZY AND COMFORTABLE WITH AWKWARD

Awkward is the price of admission
for authentic connection.
HOLLEY GERTH

When my husband and I visited a new church after moving to Colorado Springs, we decided to attend one of the Sunday school classes—or, rather, "community groups"—after the service to get a more comprehensive feel for the church and our potential place in it. After walking into the large room, David and I sat on the far-left side of the class in the second-to-top row. While other folks wandered in, my eyes scanned the room. And that's when I noticed a brown-eyed gal who I instantly—but barely—remembered from . . . somewhere? I discreetly pointed her out to David, but he didn't remember crossing paths with her or the fellow sitting next to her. I couldn't grasp any concrete memory with her in it, so I decided that she must just *look* like someone I know.

Over the next few weeks, we continued to visit that church and community group, and I continued to look at that same girl and debate with myself whether or not I knew her. While I met several folks in that class, it was sizable enough that this gal and I never came close enough in proximity to introduce ourselves to each other. So as I talked with and became acquainted with other people, I continued to reach into the furthest recesses of my mind to shake loose some kind of memory with this gal in it.

A short while later, David and I decided to officially join the church as well as this community group. On yet another Sunday, I walked in and did a sweep of the folks in the room, once again setting my sights on the gal in question. Then I sat down as our class proceeded along with the usual lesson and prayer time. At the end of class, however, our teacher brought up the subject of small groups, which were kicking off for the year. He proceeded to direct those who'd signed up for a small group, which David and I had done, to different tables, encouraging us to get to know those assigned to our group. David and I moved toward the table of the group we would be joining. As it turned out, we found ourselves sitting across from the familiar girl and her husband.

Our small group leader, Fred, asked us to go around the table and introduce ourselves. Brown-Eyed Girl introduced herself as Aimée, wife of the fellow sitting next to her, Rusty. At that moment, it was like an electric current jolted me awake with an instant, blazing flash of recognition. Unable to contain myself, I slammed my hands on the table and hollered, "OF COURSE!! YOU'RE AIMÉE WHO WE MET AT EMILY'S BIRTHDAY PARTY FIFTEEN YEARS AGO!"

Cue every head in that large room swiftly swinging my

direction as all talking ceased, bringing the room to a complete hush. I startled Aimée so much that she jumped, hitting the table with her knee.

She stared at me, brown eyes wide, and said almost like she didn't want to own it, "Uhh, yes?" And then she snapped her fingers and said, "Wait, I remember you now! You're longtime friends of Bryan and Aundrea! And you have twin sons, right?"

I grinned and nodded my head up and down. Apologizing to the whole table for my awkward outburst, I explained how I was sure I'd met Aimée and her husband before, but for weeks I couldn't place where, when, or how. But then, like a Mack truck running into my brain, I remembered that we'd met at the birthday party of a mutual friend of ours.

At the end of class, we further recounted our connections through other mutual friends and how we'd each seen the other pop up on those friends' social media accounts. We also talked about our kids and our present and future plans.

From that first moment, I enjoyed a kinship with this vivacious gal who has hype-girl energy in spades. Our friendship took off running, and it hasn't stopped since. Ten years later, Aimée has proven over and over again to be a loyal, true-blue friend who is one of my closest confidants.

What I love, too, about my friendship with Aimée is that it proves that one can display Olympic-gold levels of awkward behavior at the dawn of a friendship, and yet it's not a hindrance to the development of that friendship.

It just might serve as an encouragement to that friendship.

When trying to find friends following the pandemic, Noor Bouzidi, a journalist and producer with *New York* magazine's *The Cut*, said, "Feeling a little awkward and desperate is pretty much the starter dough of any friendship I was hoping to form."[1]

By now we know that making friends requires hard work,

and we know that desperation can drive us to consider doing a crazy thing or two in order to find them, like holding a sign in the front yard (*ahem*). Now we're going to dive headfirst into another reality we must accept: Making friends is plumb awkward.

While many of us *think* we know this fact, our actions to the contrary betray what we really believe.

Most of us readily accept that dating is awkward as can be; we don't accept that the art of making friends is awkward for ev-er-y-one. Ironically, finding friends as a grown-up is a lot like dating in that you need some form of chemistry to form a connection with the other person, even if that chemistry and connection look and feel different. Instead, we believe other women must've figured out how to get around the awkward factor, easily laughing and skipping to their girlfriend coffee dates and dinner drinks by bibbidi-bobbidi-booing their way to that connection.

But no one gets to enjoy the deep waters of a friendship without first wading through the awkward waters. It may not be as awkward as my introduction to Aimée, but meeting and getting to know new people always carries one degree of it or another.

I think this is why so many are drawn to social media as their primary source for friendship connections. Social media lets you circumvent the awkward, at least to a certain degree. That is, it's easier to foster a connection on social media with less awkwardness. By sending a text or direct message or Snap, we show up with a sliver of who we are as opposed to the totality of who we are that meeting in person requires. Because it requires less commitment, social media tricks us into believing it's infinitely more ideal because it requires less work on our part.

At the same time, its bite-sized way of communicating allows us to rein in the awkward. We can control what we say and how we come across much more than we can when we sit with someone for a couple of hours at an actual meal. However, while extended time in person may feel riskier, it also holds the potential for a much greater reward.

What's more, connection fostered *only* through social media will be more superficial and shallow. Unless some of those online connections turn into real-life ones, they're no substitute for in-person friendships.

The good news is that the more you practice pushing through the awkward, the less the awkwardness will bother you. Oh, I'm not saying it'll completely go away. I've been intentionally pursuing friendships for thirty years now, and the endeavor still carries awkward moments. But that doesn't bother me today like it used to. And that's saying something, because I used to be one who would constantly evaluate what I'd said and hadn't said in an encounter with a friend or potential friend, mentally grading myself on how well I'd maneuvered the conversation. If I'd done well, I gave myself an A. If I thought I'd come across as awkward or weird, I gave myself an F.

While I can't say I'm completely healed of this insecurity, the blessing of being the age I am is just caring less. Besides, we're all too busy worrying about what we've said to be worried about what *she* said. So all that grading myself on my friendship abilities was not only a ridiculous use of my time; it wasn't an accurate reflection of how my friends or potential friends viewed me in those encounters. Sure, someone likely did view some of my words and actions as annoying, awkward, or off-putting and therefore decided I wasn't worth their time or investment. But I've truly come to see that as okay. If someone doesn't want to be around me, they're not God's best for me (and vice versa).

Part of what has helped me accept this fact is what time and experience have shown me, which is that the awkward factor actually moves us in the direction of finding and forming friend-ships; it doesn't deter them. As a woman who ascribes to the Christian faith, I get much encouragement and direction from the Bible. Its stories are full of interactions that required one or more people to stumble through awkwardness in order to reach a relationship that blessed them.

If we flip several books into the Bible's New Testament, we read about the awkwardness that surely plagued Paul and John Mark, at least during the early part of their friendship. As told in Acts 15:35–41, Paul and Barnabas, who were ministry partners, appeared to be on the same page as to how to proceed with their journey, until a discussion about one controversial figure, John Mark (aka Mark), joining them on their travels resulted in a sharp disagreement. While Barnabas wanted to bring Mark along, Paul clearly had a problem with him. We're not exactly sure what that problem was, but it was likely over the fact that earlier on, Mark had done an about-face by withdrawing from them and the work they were doing. Perhaps Paul saw this as a serious character flaw, or he worried it was a sign of a character flaw that made Mark unsuitable for ministering alongside them.

Whatever the reason, he didn't want Mark to join them, and Paul and Barnabas couldn't agree to disagree about it. Tempers flared to such a degree that Paul and Barnabas decided to part ways, with Paul and Silas heading one direction toward Syria and Cilicia, and Barnabas and Mark heading in another direction toward Cyprus.

The interesting thing is, we read in Colossians 4:10 that Paul instructed the Christians there to welcome Mark. And we read in 2 Timothy, as Paul languished at the end of his life in a dungeon prison, that one of the few things he requested was the presence of Mark. "Get Mark and bring him with you, because he is help-ful to me in my ministry" (4:11).

Obviously, somewhere along the way Paul's heart changed toward Mark. And somewhere along the way Mark, who would go on to write one of the Gospels, proved that he was trustworthy. But I would imagine that between the time when Paul didn't trust him to when he did, he and Mark had an awkward encounter or three. And yet, Paul came to treasure Mark's presence and help with the mission.

So awkwardness that comes from a disagreement or someone's negative opinion can still lead to deep friendship. Don't let the potential or actual occurrence of an awkward encounter boss you into believing that the potential friendship isn't worth getting past the awkward. It is, every time.

If you're still unconvinced, let me leave you with one last awkward story from my personal archives.

When the air force transferred my family to Hawaii, several folks, including one of David's bosses, met us at the airport and helped us move all ten pieces of our luggage from baggage claim to our rental car. This same boss, after placing several pieces of luggage in the trunk, came around to the side of the car where I was standing by the open door of the back seat.

Suddenly, I noticed him lean down toward me, and for some inexplicable reason, I took this to mean he wanted to give me a hug goodbye. So I opened my arms and hugged him, realizing too late that he didn't want to hug me. (Of course not, because that is *weird!*) Instead, he wanted to lean down to tell the kids, who were buckled in the back seat, "Welcome to Hawaii."

Ohmahstars—my cheeks still get hot when I recollect this most awkward, embarrassing hug! Thankfully he had a sense of humor about it and didn't hold it against me.

Now, this particular boss of David's didn't become my friend, per se. But a gal named Kim, who was there and witnessed the whole awkward hug event, did become my good friend. Holy moly, we still laugh today about that time I hugged the detachment bigwig right out of the blue.

Awkward can be uncomfortable, yes. But it can also be hilarious. Either way, awkward isn't the end of the world. There's something about the way the most fledgling, awkward of beginnings can yield the most auspicious fruit in meaningful friendships.

While not every awkward introduction will lead to a friendship that sticks, every friendship that sticks includes awkward components. It's simply the quirky scenery we encounter on the path traveled from acquaintance to familiar friends. We just need to accept that—and get over ourselves enough—to believe it's worth experiencing along the way.

With practice, we'll see how the awkward factor is like hearing someone else's kid throw a fit in church: It's something you can't necessarily ignore, but it doesn't really bother you.

> While not every awkward introduction will lead to a friendship that sticks, every friendship that sticks includes awkward components.

If you sense the Holy Spirit nudging you toward a potential friend, don't let the awkward factor stop you. Introduce yourself and extend an invitation her way. And if you get together and find yourself displaying awkward behavior, take heart: You get an A for awkward in my book, and you might find that invitation leads to an awesome friendship.

HOW TO BE A GOOD FRIEND TO YOURSELF

Accept that, like dating, making friends is awkward in the beginning. But with practice, you'll see that a very awkward introduction to someone can lead to the most meaningful friendship. What's more, social media may let you circumvent the awkward, but unless those online connections turn into real-life ones, it'll circumvent deep connection too.

CHAPTER 5

BOUNDARIES ARE YOUR FRIENDS

*Daring to set boundaries is about having
the courage to love ourselves, even
when we risk disappointing others.*
BRENÉ BROWN

Whether your own wounds at the hands of "friends" happened last week or last century, they can stay with you long after the people who caused them have exited your life.

In my hometown of Ponca City, Oklahoma, I attended First Lutheran School from kindergarten through sixth grade. After graduating from that school with thirteen or fourteen of my peers, I transitioned to a huge, loud, overwhelming public middle school. Always a tall girl, twelve-year-old me resembled a giraffe amid a herd of zebras. While I relish my five-foot-ten-inch height now, I didn't much care for it then. Like a lot of seventh graders, I wanted to stay under people's radars while managing to fit in too. A full head taller than most of my peers, I did neither. I was a fish out of water, certainly no swan gliding across its surface.

So when Gail showed interest in being friends with me, I was ecstatic. I warmed up to her lightning fast, enjoying her sparkling, effervescent personality.

Gail and I talked all the time, often about boys—like who we thought was cute and looked especially good in their Guess or Wrangler jeans. Sometimes we'd share why we liked a certain boy or why we didn't.

Later, however, I noticed a change in Gail. She began to press me for specific reasons I liked someone, especially regarding a fella I had a crush on. This was well and good till her probing started to feel off. It gave me pause, or a catch in my spirit, but I brushed it off because I was so happy to have made what I thought was a good friend. *You're just being overly cautious*, I told myself. I gave Gail the benefit of the doubt because I saw no concrete reason not to.

I came to regret that decision when I discovered that Gail, who liked the same boy I did but never told me, was going to him and telling him everything I told her about him.

God bless my seventh-grade heart that would've preferred to have chewed off my own arm than to have been exposed and humiliated in that way.

One thing is for certain, though: I never told Gail another thing about a boy or anything else. She broke my trust in a profound way, and even as a young girl I understood the best way to handle that kind of betrayal was with a river-wide boundary.

While placing boundaries between Gail and myself was a no-brainer, I've lived through other situations that weren't so cut-and-dried. Honestly, I don't think of Gail much at all these days, but I do often think about another friend situation that required me to put up boundaries as well.

Eileen and I met when my twin sons were still in diapers. Eileen also had twins, and we immediately bonded over our mutual assembly-line experiences that mothering multiples presents. Eileen and I shared similar life stages, similar approaches to parenting, and an identical hunger for friends. At least we did at the beginning of our friendship.

That friendship started out swimmingly with easygoing play dates, or as much of a play date as you can have with a gaggle of babies whose ages are measured in months. But then I noticed her critical spirit moving into our conversations. It started out innocently enough with her ribbing me lightheartedly, like when she'd tease me for being picky about how I liked to brew my cup of tea. (I *am* picky about that, so that was fair.)

But with time, those kinds of comments turned more biting, and she'd say, "Her Royal Highness becomes a real b**** if her tea isn't brewed just right!"

Listen, I certainly prefer a good cup of tea, but many a time I've sat in silence and drank a poor cuppa that someone else kindly made for me. *I'm* picky about how *I* brew my tea, but I'm not going to be rude about how another person brews it for me. So when she said that, I bristled—but I didn't say anything. In fact, I laughed in order to help defuse the tension.

Furthermore, while Eileen and I often babysat each other's babies, I could tell my requests for childcare help started to grate on her nerves. One time, when I had a doctor's appointment open up for me last minute, I called and asked her if she might be willing to watch the boys during that appointment.

She sighed with such irritation that I immediately regretted asking.

"Well . . . I *guess* I can, *if* I'm your only option," she said, exasperated annoyance dripping off her every word.

As someone who'd reciprocated caring for her kids last minute myself, I felt both flummoxed and frustrated by her behavior. I moved back from the phone like I'd been slapped. I thought, *Message received, loud and clear. I'm a pain and a bother for asking.*

Wanting to disentangle myself from this uncomfortable situation, I quickly told her, "Oh no . . . never mind! I can tell you've got a lot going on, so I'll just reschedule the appointment for another time." We said our goodbyes, and that was that.

And yet, while I increasingly encountered her unavailability, she didn't mind asking me to help her out by babysitting her kids. Again, I didn't mind that to a certain degree, but given her moodiness about extending the same opportunity to me, our friendship began to feel terribly lopsided. More than that, the way she doubled down on the personal jabs about everything from my parenting to my faith made me feel just terrible, period.

Eileen continued to call me daily, sometimes just to vent about her struggles and sometimes to ask for favors. But after most conversations, I felt taken advantage of, not to mention all the needling made me feel worse about myself than I had before we talked.

Perhaps some folks are wired to handle toxic people with a grain of salt, but I'm not one of those people. And that's okay; I don't need to be! While I'm naturally bent toward giving people the benefit of the doubt, someone's pattern of passive-aggressive (and certainly aggressive-aggressive!) comments can stick to my mental ribs for a good while. So in order to have enough energy in my own tank (not to mention to preserve my own mental health), I've had to become comfortable with stricter boundaries between those folks and myself.

Still, I don't like disappointing people, and setting boundaries runs the risk of disappointing people from time to time. It helps me to remember that sometimes disappointing people is the right thing to do in order not to disappoint myself *or* the priority people (and priority responsibilities) in my life.

Concerning Eileen, I had to stop thinking this friendship would eventually become what I'd hoped: warm, nurturing, and one that reciprocated thoughtfulness and kindness. I had to accept that Eileen had a serious mean streak that enjoyed cutting me down to elevate herself. Because she lost my trust as a friend, she would also lose proximity to me.

But here's the interesting thing: Placing those boundaries between Eileen and myself felt 100 percent contrary to what I *should* do. It felt wrong and even a little rude.

Recently I discussed this very thing with my friend Holley, who is also a trained counselor and life coach. Recounting boundaries I'd recently placed between myself and a different friend, I mentioned to Holley that it so often feels awful to distance myself from others. Really, it feels terrible.

Holley replied, "Yeah . . . that's the thing about boundaries that no one really talks about: how it feels for the one laying them down. Everyone talks about the very real need for boundaries. But no one talks about how placing them feels wrong, even though it's not."

If you're like me, you want to be gracious with folks, generally speaking. Having said that, if someone is continually behaving in an ugly, demanding, belittling, rude, manipulative, or otherwise toxic way, like regularly tearing you down rather than building you up *or* making less of you to make more of herself, that is *not* okay. Be a good friend to yourself and accept that, at worst, it's likely this person isn't really a friend of yours. At best, you need a boundary between the two of you.

When I got serious about placing a boundary between Eileen and myself, she told me that that boundary didn't represent the way a Christian should behave and that I was mean.

Hogwash.

I certainly get how it can *feel* mean to those of us who're more sensitive, but it's not mean to set a boundary. What *is* mean is making less of yourself to make someone else more comfortable. Perhaps you can relate: Someone is making fun of you, and you laugh harder than anyone. What's more, when she's criticizing or questioning your choices, have you agreed with her, even if you thought she had no idea what she was talking about?

I sure have. I have advanced degrees in this kind of circus-ring maneuvering.

Truly, I can be mighty self-deprecating, so I have no problem with laughing at myself. I try not to take myself too seriously. But we both know the difference between engaging in that kind of humor versus a pattern of sabotaging ourselves so someone else won't feel uncomfortable or because it seems easier in the moment.

Sabotaging yourself *is* being mean to yourself. Putting up with grown-ups behaving like brats *is* being mean to yourself. Setting boundaries is *not*. Setting boundaries is being a good friend to yourself.

In the words of Chrystal Evans Hurst, "Because Jesus died for you, I will be kind to you. Because Jesus died for me, too, I'm going to be kind to me and set some healthy boundaries."[1]

Placing boundaries between yourself and someone else doesn't mean your heart is hardened to the other person. In fact, they mean you're doing your level best to stay tender toward them as you love them better from afar.

Of course, someone can holler, "Boundary!" because they're trying to avoid dealing with a problem that needs attention. But

I believe a lot of us women are too lenient with boundaries rather than too strict. And that's partly because when we put up boundaries that others don't like, there will be some kind of fallout.

Proverbs 18:2 says, "A fool takes no pleasure in understanding, but only in expressing his opinion" (ESV). However you decide to erect a boundary, your friend may balk at it instead of dealing with the pain that caused it. When one's foolishness is exposed, that person may choose to deny it and look away rather than see the problem for what it is.

That's okay. She doesn't have to agree with your boundary for it to be the right move on your part.

Healthy people will understand your need for boundaries. In the words of Gary Thomas, "Christians need to stop worrying about the unhealthy fallout of unhealthy people who are challenged by healthy decisions. We can't control the way someone responds, and their response isn't on us. We control our own efforts to be as loving, true, gentle, and kind as our God calls us to be as we live with healthy, God-ordained priorities."[2]

When I placed a boundary between myself and Eileen, I did my best to do so in a loving, true, gentle, and kind way. I stopped calling her as often. Our friendship predated texting, but if it had occurred later, I would've silenced text notifications from her on my phone and taken more time to answer her texts. I stopped asking her to babysit altogether. And when she asked me why I wasn't as available to her as I had been, I told her gently but truthfully, "Because I've sensed a shift in our friendship for a while now, and I think I need a bit of extra space for the foreseeable future. I certainly don't mean for that to hurt you or your feelings, and I'm very sorry if it does—and if I've done anything else to harm you in any way."

That was a truthful apology because I was sorry that our friendship looked different. I didn't want to hurt her feelings.

And as a flawed human who sins, I have no problem with apologizing for my own mistakes and oversights along the way. Yet sometimes feelings are gonna get hurt. That doesn't mean the boundary I placed between Eileen and myself was wrong. What another thinks of your boundary doesn't dictate whether you set one.

It's important to mention that when possible, the one setting a severe boundary—as in, the one who sets into motion a complete friendship breakup—needs to responsibly relay *why* they're setting it. I've been downwind of too many stories of how longtime friends are suddenly in a friendship breakup because one person decided she was done with the other. I'm not saying there's never a cause for a permanent severing of a friendship due to a betrayal or grievous, unchanging behavior. Of course there is. But, in those cases, I believe the one doing the severing needs to make it abundantly clear why it's happening. *Crystal clear.* Without a clear reason, abruptly ending a friendship overnight isn't a good look on the one doing it.

In light of that, following are some ideas for what to say as the one setting a boundary. The first few suggestions are mine, and the last several are those I've learned from working with my licensed professional counselor, Gwen Westerlund. Whatever we say to someone, the key is to relay the boundary without overexplaining ourselves (another struggle of mine). So from creek-sized to river-sized, here are some examples of ways to briefly and succinctly set a boundary, as well as some helpful prompts to reply with if there's pushback.

- "I wish I could help. My schedule simply doesn't allow it right now."
- "I'm so sorry I'm unable to provide that service. Do let me know how I might support you in the future."

- "It's not my intention to hurt you. Right now, though, you're wanting more from me than I'm able to give."
- "I'm happy to talk with you as long as the conversation is civil. I will not engage in unproductive conversation."
- "I'm sorry. It was not my intention to offend you." (For context: There's giving offense and taking offense. While you want to strive to use your words and actions to not purposely give offense, you can't help what someone else chooses to take offense over. At the end of the day, it's not necessarily up to you to correct someone who's taken offense over what you said.)
- "I'm limiting communication with you because I'm not willing to be spoken to in a disrespectful or abusive manner. I'm completely open to communicate when you're willing to have a constructive conversation." (For context: Your choice to limit your communication with the other person is a direct result of the other person's choice to carry communication too far.)
- "I've deeply valued our friendship. Over the past few months, however, things have changed, and the current state of our relationship damages my heart. Are you willing to talk about some ways we can change/improve our friendship? If not, I respect your decision, but I will need some distance."

When giving a boundary, say what you're going to say, then let the boundary speak for itself. There's no need for a lot of back-and-forth conversation about this unless you feel it's productive. If it's unproductive, refuse to keep yourself in the crazy cycle of repeating yourself over and over. If Eileen had further questioned my boundary, I would've used one of Gwen's prompts, like, "I'm limiting communication with you because I'm not willing to be spoken to in a disrespectful or abusive manner." If she'd further questioned that, I wouldn't have responded.

Boundaries don't mean we stop loving people. Sometimes, someone's choices carry the consequence of us loving them best from a distance. That's how we're kind to them *and* to ourselves. In the words of author Kaitlyn Bouchillon, "You are not a trash can."[3] You can choose to set yourself close enough to that friend who repeatedly throws garbage at you. *Or* you can take out the trash by placing a boundary between you and the one who's not treating you as you deserve to be treated.

As Gwen has taught me, a boundary is a tool that protects us from another's inappropriate or unacceptable behavior, not a tool to control that person's behavior. So when you need to set a boundary, you can relay what *you're* going to do when certain behaviors occur rather than telling the other person how she can or can't behave. This distinction is important.

When Jesus lived on this earth, He gave of Himself in more ways than the pages of the Bible could even tell. He preached and taught, held and healed others. And yet, He didn't give everyone unlimited access to Himself every moment of every day. He placed boundaries between Himself and people. While Jesus, at the proper time, did submit to the cross in obedience to His Father's plans, Scripture details those times when Christ purposefully removed Himself from those meaning to do Him harm (Matthew 12:14–15; John 8:59; John 10:39–40).

What's more, Jesus was intentional about those He chose to be His disciples: "Jesus went up on a mountainside and called to him those he wanted, and they came to him. He appointed twelve [disciples] that they might be with him and that he might send them out to preach" (Mark 3:13–14).

In this passage, we learn that Jesus chose His disciples. He didn't simply stand outside the city gate and holler, "MAY

I HAVE YOUR ATTENTION, PLEASE! I need some fellas to serve with Me in My ministry. The first twelve who let Me know they're interested will be picked!"

No. He thoughtfully and intentionally chose who would fulfill this important ministry role in His life.

If Jesus actively chose who was around Him each day, this means He also chose who wasn't. Therefore, we can choose who we are and aren't around every day too.[4]

Here's to having hearts that wisely discern when we need to give grace to someone and when we need to build a boundary between us and them. If you're consistently in the crosshairs of another's harmful, toxic behavior, here's to giving boundaries the benefit of the doubt instead of another's poor behavior. Boundaries are our friends.

HOW TO BE A GOOD FRIEND TO YOURSELF

If a friend is consistently behaving toward you in a toxic way, say yes to putting up a boundary between the two of you so you can best care for yourself and your priority people. Sometimes, someone's choices carry the consequence of loving her best from a distance.

CHAPTER 6

BOUNDARIES ARE YOUR FRIENDS' FRIENDS

Good relationships require good boundaries.
LYSA TERKEURST

Just as we're free to lay down boundaries, our friends are free to do the same. The question is, Will we respond respectfully to those boundaries or react negatively to them?

I've not only been the one to place a stricter boundary between myself and someone else; I've certainly been on the receiving end of a friend's boundary.

I think we'd have an easier time setting boundaries—and accepting those set by others—if we gave them better PR. After all, cities, counties, states, and countries have boundaries. Lots of places we move in and around every day have boundaries—like American public restrooms, thanks be to the good Lord above. Boundaries are a part of our everyday world.

My friend Christie and her husband, Todd, have the most stunning back deck that faces the whole expanse of the Rocky Mountain Front Range. Recently, I told Christie, "Listen, if you wake up and find me sitting on that back deck, don't be alarmed! I'm just soaking up that amazing view!"

Christie laughed good-naturedly, but I'm sure she'd quit laughing if she actually woke up one day and found me sitting there. That would qualify as odd behavior that would definitely breach a boundary. Unless there's an emergency, like I happen to notice her house is on fire, I wouldn't do that.

Spoken and unspoken boundaries are a part of life for each one of us. And yet, when it comes to setting relational boundaries, we either feel bad about placing them ourselves or get our feathers ruffled when someone else does. Of course, we want to place our boundaries thoughtfully and not use them as a tool to manipulate someone or to get under their skin. That would only bring further harm to the relationship. But when boundaries are used appropriately, they will help the person giving them and ultimately the person receiving them as well.

In terms of friendship, we can't be friends with everyone. We've *all* had boundaries placed between ourselves and others, whether we knew about them or not. This is fine when our boundaries are mutual in that we agree on their placement. In those instances, we probably give no thought to the boundaries. My friend Aimée and I have talked about an idea she introduced me to: active friendships versus passive friendships. If you and a friend both think of each other as a passive friend—an acquaintance you'll chat amiably with when the opportunity arrives but don't go out of your way to socialize with—again, no problem.

However, I've struggled with this when, a few years ago, someone I deeply cherished as an active friend suddenly put me in the category of a passive friend. I knew this because not only did she begin communicating with me less, but her messages became very short. If she texted, it was "dry texting." If I asked her a few questions about how her week was or how the kids were doing, she'd respond succinctly, "It was fine," or "They're doing well." There'd be no reciprocating questions for me.

For a while, I continued to reach out to her as I'd done before. But when I clued in to the fact that she wasn't doing the same in return, I realized that our friendship had changed. This saddened and disappointed me, to be sure. But in this case, I sensed that this wasn't due to a problem that required an apology on my part. It wasn't due to a problem on her end that I had a direct part in creating. I felt in my spirit that for her, our friendship as it was had simply run its course. And there was nothing for me to do about it but respect her decision through accepting that change—and asking God to bless her going forward, even if it was painfully obvious that I couldn't be a part of her life as I'd been before.

In time, I came to appreciate that boundary—and others I've received as well—because they provide the gift of information. Before the boundary, I thought things were one way. The boundary let me see more clearly how things were, not how I thought they were.

And that's how some friendships go over time: They simply change, and both people must accept the adjusted boundaries that come with new territory.

Nedra Glover Tawwab, bestselling author and licensed therapist, reminds us that it's easier to see when others violate our boundaries than it is to see how we may be violating theirs.[1] Nedra mentions some of the ways we may be disrespecting others' boundaries, which I've paraphrased here:

- Sharing confidences with others
- Making demands on another's time

- Refusing to give space that's been requested
- Telling someone how to feel instead of asking them how they feel
- Ignoring a clearly stated boundary[2]

I'd add "doubling down on communication" to that list.

As I said, we all experience boundaries between ourselves and others just as surely as we experience boundaries in our physical world. But if you start to feel like your friendships across the board hold a bunch of boundaries that seem beyond the run-of-the-mill kind, it may be worth the self-evaluation to see if your own habits and behaviors need to be adjusted or changed too.

I've certainly needed to do this from time to time. Some behaviors, when frequently repeated, will cause someone to put up a boundary. Here are some examples:

- Having a suspicious demeanor and not giving others the benefit of the doubt
- Talking more than listening
- Hijacking or redirecting the conversation back to you
- Bringing a self-centered agenda into the conversation
- Showing a lack of regard or sensitivity to the other person's circumstances
- Caring more about airing your opinion than listening respectfully
- Gossiping frequently (Today we call it "spilling the tea," which often is just gossiping in a cute skirt.)

I was not born with an abundance of interpersonal skills, and I didn't discover and learn them until the military life gave me a baptism-by-fire education in what works—and doesn't work—to make friends. I'm certainly guilty of overreaching in a friendship and disrespecting another person's boundaries myself. In His kindness, God has worked on my heart *a lot* in this area. Also, He's put women around me who modeled boundaries and friendship in a way I wanted to emulate. These friends don't gossip, so I know they're not talking ugly about me when I'm not around. They give folks the benefit of the doubt, so I know they won't get huffy if I have to change plans at the last minute. And they certainly don't balk at creating boundaries or respecting those set by others.

If I had a scheduled coffee or dinner date with a friend, but my day had gone sideways and I knew I didn't have the energy or desire for extra socializing, I used to tell myself that a good friend muscles through and keeps the dinner date, regardless of how zapped she is. An example of this was when I was both mama to infant twin babies and a public-school elementary teacher. One week, a dear teacher friend of mine, Patty, invited me to a scrapbooking party at her house that Friday evening. (We Gen Xers used to loooooove scrapbooking our hearts out!) By that Friday afternoon, I felt exhausted. The twins hadn't slept well the night before, and after teaching all morning, I was running on fumes. I told Patty that despite telling her I could go, I didn't think I'd be able to after all. I began to run down the list of reasons I couldn't make it, each followed by profuse apologies, when she put her hand up to cut me off.

"Kristen," she said, "being a person—especially a mama with babies—means plans are going to change. It's okay to cancel plans from time to time. Good friends know this, accept this, and understand that now and then, we all must say no to a good thing to say yes to a better thing."

While Patty relayed that she'd miss me that night, she respected my boundary—and showed me how to respect others' boundaries too.

Friends like Patty can show you how to set boundaries in healthy ways. Other friends can show you where you need to set a boundary in your own behavior too.

Several years ago, my friend Jen told me that I was starting to complain *a lot*. At first, I smarted at her revelation. But when I took the time to think about it, I saw that she was right. There's no denying that people who constantly complain are draining. And I saw that if I didn't get a handle on it, she—if not others too—would begin to put up a boundary between herself and me (if she hadn't already!).

I genuinely appreciated her telling me about my own propensity for complaining, because with my blind spot to this behavior removed, she put me in a better position to be a better friend.

Beth Moore writes, "Do we feel justified in constantly airing our negative opinions? Are we virtually impossible to please? Are we speaking out in bitterness of soul? Sooner or later, if we're harboring bitterness, it will bubble to the surface."[3]

Instead of letting our own negative interpersonal skills bubble to the surface in a way that causes another person to set a boundary, let's acknowledge them and deal with them so we can be the kind of friend we want to have.

It's easier to accept other people's boundaries—however they came to be—when we learn to see those boundaries in a healthier light. Here are some ways I've learned to better accept another's boundary:

- If I balk at a boundary, my pride is usually involved. So I tell my pride to stand down. I'm not entitled to be friends with another person just because I'd like to be.
- Boundaries are so often tied to a person's bandwidth, not you or me. Making boundaries about a person's bandwidth

makes it easier for me to accept. If someone's placed a boundary, it simply means I fall outside her bandwidth, just like others fall outside my own.

- I do my best to understand the situation from her point of view. There's a poem by Brian A. "Drew" Chalker that includes the line, "People come into your life for a reason, a season, or a lifetime."[4] That could easily be attributed to friends as well. It takes two people to agree on which one of those categories the friendship falls into. And if they can't agree, then the one with the stricter boundaries is the one who dictates which one it is.

- As I've written before, I remember the wise words of my dear friend Salena Duffy: "Sometimes, rejection is God's protection against what isn't in my best interest." If someone is rejecting my friendship through a boundary, it's not in my best interest.

Where I fall in relation to someone else's boundaries ain't my business. I'm not going to think ill of someone when I fall outside her boundary lines or bandwidth. I'm not going to beat myself up by saying, "Well, Kristen, this must mean there's something wrong with you." It means no such thing. It just means we all have limited resources that require us to say no to people in one way or another.

In its simplified form, a boundary is just one way of letting another person know how available you are to her. Sometimes, a change in behavior is enough to convey a boundary. At other times, words are helpful. Oftentimes, words are a *must*.

No matter what, boundaries are our friends—and our friends' friends.

> In its simplified form, a boundary is just one way of letting another person know how available you are to her.

HOW TO BE A GOOD FRIEND TO YOURSELF

Boundaries are simply the easiest way to communicate how much access we get from one another. Just as everyone can't have unlimited access to you, you can't have unlimited access to them. Be thankful for boundaries because they offer clarifying information to you.

CHAPTER 7

BELIEVE IN SURPRISE
FRIENDSHIPS

A friend may be waiting
behind a stranger's face.
MAYA ANGELOU, *LETTER TO MY DAUGHTER*

For the first year of our marriage, David and I lived in a small apartment in Middletown, Ohio. We chose Middletown because—true to its name—it was halfway between where David worked and where I went to school. On a regular, nothin'-special day in late spring, while driving up I-675 to work at Wright-Patterson Air Force Base, my husband noticed a man walking alongside the busy interstate.

David has no problem offering a ride to a hitchhiker as long as the circumstances present no red flags. After noticing that this freeway fella wore a USAF uniform and had a vehicle close to where he was walking, David pulled over and asked if he could help. David learned that the other guy, Joe, had run out of gas, so David offered to take him to a gas station off Wilmington Pike, the next closest exit. Once Joe gratefully accepted and had his gas can full of fuel, David dropped him off at his car, where Joe continued to thank him for the ride and the help. Then David drove to work, and Joe, after filling up his car with gas, did the same.

That evening, David came home and told me about his turn as the good Samaritan. I smiled at the story, proud that my man was a helper kind of person. Then, both of us put that encounter on the back shelf of our thoughts.

That is, until a few weeks later.

When I was no longer in school full-time, David and I had rented a townhouse in a suburb of Dayton that placed us much closer to the base and all the advantages it offered. We had signed the lease for it well before David met Joe on the side of the freeway. Yet, imagine David's surprise—not to mention Joe's—when six weeks later, we moved into the same townhouse complex as Joe and his wife, JulieAnne. Not only were we in the same complex; we were only two doors down from them in the same building.

As I've previously mentioned, it took me a while to make friends as a newlywed. We met Joe and JulieAnne in the second year of our marriage, and David and I took to them like a fly to flypaper. They were hilarious, engaging, and genuine as all get-out. We also got a kick out of our personality and regional differences. Joe and JulieAnne were from the East Coast, and David and I were from Middle America. They rooted for the Philadelphia Eagles. We cheered for the Dallas Cowboys. Each couple chuckled at the other's accents—while both were 100 percent sure *we* didn't have an accent nearly as strong as the other's.

(Joe and JulieAnne, I maintain that your accents *are* much stronger than mine.)

JulieAnne possessed a no-nonsense, tell-it-like-it-is way of communicating, yet she wasn't unkind at all. I carried a pervasive fear of hurting someone's feelings, so my words were heavily filtered. JulieAnne didn't have much time or patience for emoting, whereas I gushed emotion in every conversation. She was five years older than me and, like her husband, had a well-rounded worldview that extended past their driveway. I was a fifth-year college senior who still had a lot of maturing to do.

JulieAnne immediately impressed me with her witty, smart self, and the four of us got along like a house afire. We proceeded to log a lot of hours together at Super Bowl parties, double dates at Cozymel's Mexican Grill, and weekend visits at any one of Ohio's many summer and fall festivals. And since David and I didn't have cable but Joe and JulieAnne did, they let me regularly come over to watch *Beverly Hills, 90210* and *Melrose Place*—even though they, as medical residents, were endlessly exhausted from marathon shifts at their respective hospitals.

My memory bank still bulges at the seams with all the good memories the four of us made together. And it's *such* a testament to God's grace that of "all the gin joints in all the towns in all the world," to borrow Humphrey Bogart's words from *Casablanca*, we ended up right next to them. I'm not a believer in coincidences. Coincidences don't just happen; they're given. Meeting Joe and JulieAnne was no mere coincidence but divine providence graciously giving us an early taste of meaningful friendship that has only deepened with time—even though we haven't lived in the same city since 1997.

Some friendships take time, yes. But sometimes they can show up as quick as a finger snap when you least expect them. Because of this, we want to leave room for the expectancy of a surprise friendship in our lives.

But like all friendships, even surprise ones that are divinely arranged can run into troubling territory.

By the time I met Joe and JulieAnne, I'd learned a few skills in how to make friends, but once I was out of school full-time, my opportunities for employing those skills were few and far between. I spent my days working part-time and commuting to the university's two satellite campuses, so I spent a little time in a lot of places. Developing friendships, while not impossible, was still tricky.

On top of that, I carried the mindset that since I had Joe and JulieAnne as friends, I didn't need to work too hard to find others. This might've been fine if I'd had a healthier concept of boundaries. But with a mountain of insecurities and a needy side to my personality, I made mistakes with Joe and JulieAnne. *A lot.*

Mainly, I overwhelmed them.

While I was busy with both work and school, my husband was gone much of the time. So when Joe and JulieAnne gave me attention, like inviting me over for dinner, I gobbled that invitation right up and extended three more their direction. This in itself isn't terrible, but it can come across as too much. Sometimes I came across as not simply asking for seconds but ransacking their cupboards for more of their time. As one who's been on the receiving end of that behavior, I can say it's mighty obnoxious.

It wasn't till I began my year of student teaching that my schedule and time became rather consumed, and those circumstances forced me to give Joe and JulieAnne more breathing room in our friendship.

This part of my friendship history could've easily gone into chapter 6 on boundaries or chapter 9 on expectations, or even chapter 18 about forgiving mistakes. But I put it here to show that even though a friendship can surprise you with the ease in which it comes together, it will still require work and a lot of grace to see it through. *All* stages of *all* friendships require both work and grace. At the same time, your surprise friendship may not require the work mine did. You may be miles ahead of me in maturity. But we'd do well to avoid the kind of thinking that says, *Because this friendship is meant to be, it'll be problem-free.* No relationship is problem-free. But Lord willing, we get better at handling problems as they arise—and doing the work on ourselves in the first place so we cut problems off at the pass.

The remarkable thing about my friendship with Joe and JulieAnne, particularly with JulieAnne, is that she had Job-like patience with me while being out-of-this-world kind. She didn't treat me as a nuisance or a numbskull, a burden or a bother. She didn't drop a single hint that I was overwhelming—at least not one I picked up on. She wasn't dramatic or victim-y about my behavior. She just held tight to her boundaries, like saying no to my invites that didn't work for her or maintaining that we didn't need to talk or see each other on the daily just because we were neighbors. At the same time, she made room in her life for me as she had the room.

With time, I chilled out, backed the heck off, and eventually caught up to her maturity-wise. Then we were both free to enjoy the ebb and flow of an easy, no-demands friendship. But I'll always be thankful that JulieAnne gave me gobs of grace and stuck it out with me during a time when she'd have been justified to do the opposite.

It was like JulieAnne could see the future me and thought it was worth sticking it out for when that person eventually showed up.

In Joshua 3, we read about how the Israelites, after a forty-year trek across the desert, were finally going to cross the Jordan River into the land God had promised to them. Getting an army of forty thousand people across the football-field-wide river was no small feat. Since it was harvest and the river was at flood stage (v. 15), it's believed that it was ten feet deep or even deeper.[1] But God had a plan for getting them across, and He shared it with Joshua.

Joshua said to the Israelites,

> Come here and listen to the words of the LORD your God. This is how you will know that the living God is among you. . . . See, the ark of the covenant of the Lord of all the earth will go into the Jordan ahead of you. Now then, choose twelve men from the tribes of Israel, one from each tribe. And as soon as the priests who carry the ark of the LORD—the Lord of all the earth—set foot in the Jordan, its waters flowing downstream will be cut off and stand up in a heap. (vv. 9–13)

Forty years earlier, the Lord had parted the Red Sea for the Israelites so they could escape their Egyptian captors. And when He parted the Red Sea, it had parted *immediately*. However, as the priests now stepped into the river water with the ark of the covenant—the special chest that was the place of God's presence—the waters didn't immediately part right in front of them as they had for their ancestors who'd crossed the Red Sea. When the priests set foot in the Jordan River, God dammed up the waters "a great distance away," twenty to thirty miles upriver from the Israelites (vv. 15–16). So it took time for the waters to stop flowing downstream where the priests and other Israelites stood.

But eventually, the waters did stop. "The priests who carried the ark of the covenant of the LORD stopped in the middle of the Jordan and stood on dry ground, while all Israel passed by until the whole nation had completed the crossing on dry ground" (v. 17).

It took time for the Israelites to see that while they waited downstream, God was working upstream. Eventually, though, their faith became sight, and they could see how God was moving on their behalf all along—even before they could see it in the moment.

About this passage, author Priscilla Shirer writes,

> From your current vantage point, you may not be able to see how God is working out His purposes in your life . . . Life just seems to roll on like always before, oblivious to your prayers and to the faith you've placed in God's ability to change things. But be convinced that even though God may be working "a great distance away," He is working. He hasn't forgotten about you or His promises to you. . . . The [answer] may be far away from your sight and impossible as of yet to detect, but be assured that the mighty hand of God's power is already at work on your behalf.[2]

Dear one, if you're scanning the horizon for friends and don't yet see who you'd like to see, don't believe that's because God is absent and doesn't care about you and your loneliness. We spend much of our lives downstream in the mud and the muck, completely unaware of what's happening upstream. But God is in both places, and He loves us enough to ensure that even if we see no positive change where we are, "the mighty hand of God's power is already at work on [our] behalf." From where I stand downstream, I can look back at my history and see how God has provided for me in my friendships, even when what I saw in front of me looked, felt, and sounded contrary to that.

Often, we can't see how God is moving in our lives till after the fact. God arranged the circumstances for David and me to meet Joe and JulieAnne well before they were on our radar. Yes, we might have become friends with them even if David hadn't paid attention to that nudge to pull over and give Joe a ride. But because he did, and because we all met up at the same pinpoint dot on a map in Kettering, Ohio, we couldn't deny the directional arrows pointing to the fact that our friendship was meant to be.

Thirty years later, no matter how much time has passed since our communication, we can call or text one another and pick right back up like we talked ten minutes ago.

Romans 4:17 tells of how "God . . . gives life to the dead and calls into existence the things that do not exist" (ESV). Yes, a slow-growing friendship could suddenly meet a good dose of Miracle-Gro, causing it to grow like gangbusters. A friendship—or the makings of a friendship—could appear right off the side of the road as you're driving along, turning an ordinary Wednesday into a memory marker forever.

God hasn't forgotten about your real and valid need for friends, and He's already working on your behalf to that end. Anything He orchestrates upstream will cascade its way downstream to you. And if you fear your choices or someone else's have permanently damaged a friendship, take heart. If God can make the waters stop, He can make them reverse course too. Either way, He will make a way for you to walk from where you are to the people He has for you.

HOW TO BE A GOOD FRIEND TO YOURSELF

God moved to bring Joe and JulieAnne into our lives well before David and I were aware of them. God delights in surprising us with friendships that take little to no work to formulate. But that doesn't mean they won't take work (and grace) to maintain. Be a good friend to yourself by remembering that God is always working upstream in your life to give you the friends you need. Today, God is working toward your future friendships.

CHAPTER 8

WHEN FINDING FRIENDS TAKES FOREVER, ASK YOURSELF THESE QUESTIONS

For a few of us there will always be a
tugging at the heart—knowing a precious
moment gone and we not there. We can
ask and ask but we can't have again
what once seemed ours forever.
J. L. CARR, *A MONTH IN THE COUNTRY*

didn't realize till we moved to Colorado Springs and decided to stay for the long haul that it could still take a long time to make friends even if you *aren't* moving regularly. After living here several years, I had such a thin community that if you held it up to the light, you could see right through it.

Upon moving to Colorado Springs, we delightedly met up with friends we'd made earlier through David's military career. Like a collection of mountain peaks in the Rocky Mountain Front Range, we'd all circled around and landed ourselves in Colorado Springs (or "the Springs" if you want to sound local). So when we arrived there during the height of summer, we slid right back into deep life with those familiar friends as easily as we would our favorite, comfy T-shirts.

After twenty-six years of frequently pulling up stakes in his military service, David was ready to let roots grow under our feet. The kids and I didn't argue with that plan. We were happy to plant ourselves in a town drenched in sunshine and splendor. We were thrilled to be not only where David could find employment on the civilian side of the fence, but where we knew people who were staying put too.

For several years, we felt like we'd slid into home plate after hitting a locational home run. But eventually, change came along and switched that up. A couple of those good friends moved. Another found a full-time job. My relationship with a couple of other friends changed. One day, I looked around and realized, *When you stay in one place long enough, you can still lose your friends—or at least be lonely for the way things used to be.*

I still had a couple of other friends, but we didn't see each other often because they lived a long way from my neighborhood. Other changes came too. My family and I were still in the process of hunting for a church home. At the same time, family responsibilities, including raising children in elementary and middle school, made me busier than ever. I also worked from home when the kids were at school, and after school I lived that chauffeur-mama life, driving my darlings hither and yon to their activities. In addition, my dad's declining health and other relational turmoil weighed heavily on me.

While I still had and certainly enjoyed the presence of my family and our active life, it felt like someone had put the components of my life in a box and shaken it. From the outside looking in, nothing appeared different. On the inside, however, much had changed. Without the saturated color that girlfriends provide, life felt more like a muted photograph.

I wasn't bored—show me a mama in the thick of parenting, and I'll show you a woman who wishes she had the luxury of boredom. I was just lonesome for the kind of company that only good girlfriends provide. I made time to call and catch up with friends who lived out of town, and I shared with them about the last time my loved one frustrated the heck out of me, or my worry over another loved one's trajectory. And while those kinds of conversations are helpful, they're not quite as helpful as being able to talk face-to-face, one heart taking in the other's.

Simply put, I missed the way things used to be.

Eventually, time did what time does, and I saw the sun peek out from behind the clouds by way of a positive change in my friendship circumstances. We joined a new church, and the kids transitioned to middle school and high school. Both those realities put me in the path of new people and provided at least the potential for starting new friendships.

And yet, it still took more time to form real friendships because God's timing can't be hurried and connections can't be forced.

If I'm being honest, though, I can now see how I contributed to the problem by not setting myself up for success. Here are some ways I was not a good friend to myself during that time:

1. **SINCE I HAD FRIENDS, I DIDN'T THINK I NEEDED NEW FRIENDS.** For most of our air force moves, we showed up where we didn't know anyone—or at least not well. Because we

arrived in Colorado Springs where friends already lived, I rested heavily on those friends. In other words, I didn't do anything to make *new* friends. Oh, sure, I met plenty of new people. I attended events or dinners that offered a likelihood of connecting with more folks. But instead of leaning into that, I kicked back with the friends I had, and I didn't worry much about widening my circle to include new people.

But then those friendships changed, and I saw how if I'd only invested effort in getting to know new people back then, I wouldn't have found myself in such poor shape at that point in time. So I asked myself, *What can I do to lean into new potential friendship connections without sacrificing those I already have?* I learned I could keep my heart open to a new connection, because we never know when the Lord wants to do a new thing in our lives! We never know when God may graciously want to bring us a new friend, so we shouldn't close our hearts off to the idea, no matter how ideal we think our friendship situation looks.

2. **I MISTOOK KNOWING A LOT OF PEOPLE FOR HAVING A LOT OF FRIENDS.** By the time we moved to Colorado Springs, I knew a lot of people. A *lot*. But somewhere in my mind, I translated that into believing this also meant I had a lot of friends. If this was true, I had another reason not to reach out to new people. I realized, though, that while I knew folks—and had friends—across the globe, I didn't have many in Colorado Springs. And I certainly didn't have many I felt I could be vulnerable with.

Author Drew Hunter has wisely written, "Friendship should be more like a submarine, holding few and going deep. But we've made it more like a cruise ship, filled with lots of nice people whom we don't know well at all."[1]

None of us needs (or likely wants) a few hundred friends. A "friend" on Facebook or the acquaintance you see at your kids' school doesn't translate into an actual friendship. Our active friends are those we can go deep with, and we can't go deep with more than a few folks.

So that led me to ask an important question: *How am I defining friendship?*

If I'm defining every acquaintance as a friend, I'm defining friendship wrong. And if I'm refusing to be vulnerable with any friend, it's no wonder I feel I don't have any. Your level of friendship satisfaction is equivalent to the level of depth you're willing to travel with your friend or friends. If you have fifty friends you're simply milling about the surface with, sharing all manner of small talk, you'll feel much less satisfied. On the other hand, if you have only one genuine friend with whom you visit the water's depths—like your real, noncute parenting struggles, relational difficulties, and struggles with sin— you'll feel more satisfied in your friendships.

Perhaps it's hard for you to share from the deep because of your own insecurities. Or perhaps you had well-meaning older relatives who held tight to the mantra, "Never air your dirty laundry." It's inappropriate, even shameful to do such a thing, or so they said. Well, I've come to learn there ain't a thing wrong with airing some dirty laundry. Now, I'm typically not interested in doing that in a social media post for the cruise-ship masses to see. And there are parts of me and my life I share only with God. But it's far from inappropriate for us to trust a couple of friends with our dirty laundry. By and large, they won't be shocked by what we share. They'll be relieved and encouraged because we all have some dirty laundry we wouldn't mind unburdening our-selves of.

I want to mention here that while it's true you can't go deep with the cruise-ship masses, I believe it's best to have more than one person you can go deep with so you don't unintentionally overwhelm a submarine friend. You don't need a lot of those active submarine friendships, but it's best to have a couple of them.

If I had defined friendship earlier and with more intention, I could've saved myself the sad reality of going without friends as long as I did.

3. I WANTED EASY OVER EFFORT. I struggled to *want* to reach out as I'd done before. I'd gone submarine deep with a few friends who lived in town, as well as out-of-state and across the world. We shared history, and they knew the good, bad, and ugly that made up Kristen Strong. Instead of wanting to get back on the horse by way of investing in other women and risking vulnerability with them, I retreated.

As my friend Lisa-Jo Baker once put it, I felt too tired to "catch new people up on my old stuff." And listen, that exhausted feeling was fair. For years and years, I expended untold amounts of energy in an effort to make friends—to "catch people up" on the depths of my life.

It was easy to go deep with the gals who were already my friends when we moved to the Springs. But now those friendships had changed. As time went on and the door potentially opened to others, I found myself second-guessing how deep I could go with them. So I asked myself, *Do I want easy, or do I want friends?* I wanted friends. Therefore, I needed to do the hard things of reaching out, risking vulnerability, and possibly facing rejection. I could acknowledge my exhaustion over the whole ordeal, because making friends *is* tiring. But I couldn't let it boss me into doing something that sabotaged what was best for me.

This naturally leads to another important component of friendships that makes pursuing them and investing in them harder, not easier. Dr. Timothy Keller stated,

In the real world of relationships, it is impossible to love people with a problem or a need without in some sense sharing or even changing places with them. . . . It may be that they may feel stronger and more affirmed as you talk, but that won't happen without you being quite emotionally drained yourself. It's them or you. To bring them up emotionally you must be willing to be drained emotionally.[2]

I wondered, *What if I drain myself on behalf of the other person—even receiving a bang-up friendship in return—and then they up and leave too? What if I have to start over again? Is it worth the risk of working so hard to have it come to nothing?*

I stood at a crossroads not unlike the one I faced during my early twenties when I'd had no experience in making friends. Now I was back here because I was haggard from the effort it required. While that was true, it was also true that I wanted all the benefits of a friendship without the work.

As with anything of value in this world, long-term friendships come with the price tag of sacrifice. With a fresh acceptance of this fact, I began initiating friend invites again as well as saying yes when others invited me to do something. Not all those meetups resulted in a meaningful friendship, but a small number of them did. Because of that, I relearned that friendship is worth the work and the sacrifice.

Whether your reason for going a long time without friends looks similar to or different from mine, most of us will have seasons without friends. And it bears mentioning that there could be another reason we unwillingly face unwanted seasons without friends. There are times when the Lord, in His knows-all-things wisdom, *temporarily* winnows one area of our lives to widen our focus on another. If you sense this in your own life right now, it won't be the case forever. The Lord never wants us to walk around without friends indefinitely. But we may be asked to for a season because He wants to call our attention to something that needs tending to. What that could be is as diverse as the people it applies to. But we each need to ask ourselves, *Where does God want my attention right now?*

In my past, it's been because the Lord wanted me to deal with some personal things either in my heart or in my relationship with Him or others. Experiencing leaner friendships helped meet that need by removing some of my distractions.

As with so many hardships of life, ranging from silly to very serious, I could see how God permitted something undesirable to accomplish that which was very desirable.[3] God always goes for the long game, so we know He'll never sell us short by asking us to go through a rough friendship season for no reason.

I eventually did find a good family of friends again. I won't pretend it happened quickly—it did not. But it did happen. Ecclesiastes 3:1 tell us, "There is an appointed time for everything" (NASB). Thanks be to the good Lord above that while there's an appointed time for friendship droughts to begin, there's also an appointed time for them to end.

What's more, that friendship drought brought a lot of positive too. I learned to a greater extent that finding and maintaining friendships requires active participation and perseverance. I relearned that we never fully "arrive" at Friendship Town; we keep walking the winding road with others who are with us for however short or long that road is. I learned that reflection on my friendships is a positive direction to travel rather than squatting on the false promises of playing the victim.

Overall, I'm quite content today with the state of my friendships. (Of course, the moment I say that I feel like the devil might say, "Hold my beer.") And yet, I like to consider these questions (and others throughout this chapter) in my personal journal or prayer time:

- Am I disregarding or ignoring any friends I already have because I'm busy lamenting those I no longer have?
- Am I repeatedly making excuses to reject an invitation and therefore sabotaging my opportunity to make friends?
- When was the last time I extended an invitation to a friend or potential friend?
- Could I be going through this less-than-ideal friendship season because the Lord wants my attention elsewhere and has therefore removed distractions?
- Am I approaching my friendships with a relaxed nature, or do I, in an effort to connect, overtly or inadvertently put pressure on others by asking them to give more of themselves than they have resources to give?
- Am I struggling to be vulnerable with my close friends?
- Am I settling for ease over effort?

While we may temporarily be lean in friendships, that shouldn't be the status quo. It shouldn't be that way forever and ever, amen. God's heart is for you and me to have our people, so rest assured our seasons of meager friendships will end. And while we wait for them to end, let's not give up on finding friends or doing the work required to find them—including asking ourselves the right, helpful questions. God designed us for friendship at every age and life stage. I won't stop befriending people, because Jesus won't stop befriending me. Let's expect Him to come through.

HOW TO BE A GOOD FRIEND TO YOURSELF

There are a hundred different reasons you must sometimes endure a season without friends. For example, the Lord temporarily winnows one area of your life to widen your focus on another. So if you're in that season now, know it's normal. And if you're willing to evaluate why it may be happening through helpful questions—as well as not choose ease over effort—it won't last forever.

PART 2

HOW TO BE A GOOD FRIEND TO OTHERS

Simple principles and practices to help you grow
and deepen your friendships with others.

CHAPTER 9

WHAT YOU CAN EXPECT WILL KILL YOUR FRIENDSHIPS

I will always desperately try to get from other people what I fear God will not provide for me.
LYSA TERKEURST

Nothing has done more damage to my friendships than my propensity for setting meteorically high expectations and volleying them at someone else. Thankfully, nothing has helped supercharge my friendships more than becoming aware of this propensity and behaving differently.

When David and I were dating, I got to know his childhood best friend, Bryan, and Bryan's wife, Aundrea. Bryan and Aundrea, who married on the same day as David and me but one year earlier, graciously welcomed me into their lives. Between their wedding and ours, David and I visited Bryan and Aundrea, a military couple themselves, a few times at their home in Austin, Texas. In that same Texas town, Aundrea generously helped David plan his surprise marriage proposal to me on a charming wooden footbridge at Zilker Park. After I said "Yes!" David and I walked off that footbridge and greeted Aundrea and Bryan, who'd appeared with champagne and glasses to celebrate.

As I subsequently planned a wedding during my junior year of college, Aundrea let me bounce endless questions about marriage and military life off her. When I contemplated staying at Oklahoma State University to complete my senior year instead of transferring schools, which would've meant a year away from David, she advised me against it.

"If it's at all possible, start your marriage together. The military will separate you enough," she said.

Logistically, that proved to be one difficult choice, since transferring colleges as a senior ain't simple. Plus, I loved being at Oklahoma State. Nonetheless, transferring colleges was the right choice for me and my marriage, and I'm grateful for her advice.

Aundrea continued to be wise, kind, and openhanded with her time. So when she called six months after David and I had moved to Dayton, Ohio, to tell me that she and Bryan would be moving there as well, I hollered so loudly that she yanked the phone from her ear.

Finally, I thought, *I'll have a real-deal friend in Ohio!*

Bryan and Aundrea arrived, and gosh if David and I didn't enjoy hanging out with them. All went swimmingly for a good while as we enjoyed dinner dates and spending time at a mutually favorite spot, the Books&Co bookstore. But then circumstances revealed just how many expectations I'd carried into my friendship with Aundrea.

Aundrea rightly began making new friends while I didn't. What I *did* do was make demands on her time, and I didn't hide my annoyance if she spent time with her other friends. What's more, I felt exasperated and disappointed when she didn't share her own frustrations and fears with me to the degree that I did with her, and I let her know it.

Not surprisingly, this was likely because her chief frustration was . . . you know . . . *me*.

As I alluded to in the introduction, I was never the Regina George kind of mean girl. That's not to say I've never behaved in a mean way to friends, but I don't have a historical pattern of meanness toward people. And yet, Aundrea is Exhibit A from my history that shows how I *have* been the needy girl, expecting friends to serve as my be-all, end-all, give-me-all-so-I-feel-filled-up humans.

And this inclination is the chief way I've been a *bad* friend, or at least a difficult one to be around. I could bring the "extra" in epic proportions.

As a part-time student, a part-time employee at a clothing store, and a part-time church attendee at that point of my life, I visited several places each week, but not long enough to figure out how to connect with others in each place.

So when Aundrea descended on Dayton, I descended on her faster than a duck on a June bug. I expected Aundrea to fill all my loneliness and homesickness as a sort of friend-savior, and that's too much pressure for anyone to endure. Naturally, this led to Aundrea distancing herself by setting some stricter boundaries between us.

Ann Voskamp writes, "Expectations kill relationships."[1] It's death by strangulation as, slowly but surely, unreasonable expectations smother the everlovin' daylights out of the other person.

If we want to be a good friend, we have to keep unreasonable expectations out of our friendship experiences.

In his book *Made for Friendship*, Drew Hunter wisely advises us to consider the friends in our lives as travelers of various lanes in proximity to our own. Doing this not only keeps our expectations in check, but it helps us stay sensitive—and less reactive—to other people's changing boundaries. He writes,

> You may consider Dave a close friend who travels with you in your left lane. But then you realize that he doesn't see it this way. You're the one initiating all of the conversations. You expect him to spend a lot of time with you, but he expects much less. He's *your* close friend, but you're not *his*. What do you do? His view of you may change over time, but you have to adjust your expectations for now. If he pictures you in his middle lane, you may need to start picturing yourself that way too. Otherwise, if you force your friends to adjust to your expectations, they may take the next exit.[2]

Because I tried to force Aundrea to adjust to my expectations, she understandably headed toward the exit.

So regarding expectations, how do you—unlike myself years ago—help yourself be a good friend to others? If you sense your friend is changing to a less committed lane within your friendship, you change your lane too. The friend in the less committed lane controls the map for where the friendship is headed and how fast or slowly it gets there.

You certainly don't hop in her car, grab her steering wheel, and jerk her over into your lane. Instead, you model grace and freedom that says, *My heart has an open door, and friends taking up space in my heart are free to come and go. As with any relationship, both people get a say in what it looks like. I will not attempt to control the other person's choices or actions through unreasonable expectations. I will carry a posture of relaxed comradery.*

While my friendship with Aundrea struggled because of my

unreasonable expectations, it's well and good to have reasonable ones. From Aundrea's point of view, it was reasonable of her to expect me not to be demanding of her time.

Reasonable expectations aren't the problem. Unreasonable ones are.

By God's grace, Aundrea and I are still friends today. After a year of not speaking too much, I extended an olive branch by way of a baby gift for her first daughter. I told her how sorry I was for my behavior, and she forgave me. I'd learned more about how to be a good friend to others in that time by not carrying expectations, and she found that my changed behavior backed up my words. Then it was like God had scrubbed an eraser over the friendship's past, and we were able to start fresh.

Aundrea and I are proof that one's poor choices earlier in a friendship don't have to define it later on.

As I discovered through a different relationship that *didn't* stand the test of time, friendships can break down because of the more gradual, subtle placement of expectations.

On a busy Friday morning much more recently, I looked at my phone and saw a friend's message come through: "Hey, do you want to grab coffee today? I'd love to get together!"

While I enjoyed hanging out with this friend, doing so had become difficult. At the time, she had two adult kids to my three elementary- and middle-school ones. She didn't work inside or outside the home, and I worked part-time from home. My calendar had slivers of availability for meeting, while her schedule seemed more cavernous. Still, meet we did on many occasions. Just not as many occasions as she would've liked.

Yet I noticed a pattern where the more I relayed my unavailability, the more she texted about getting together. I felt squeezed and pressured, torn between desperately not wanting to hurt her feelings and the strong desire to face facts: I couldn't give her the level of friendship she wanted. And while I never ghosted her, certainly, I began to take longer to respond to her texts. Eventually, our separations extended for such a long period that we only communicated sporadically.

And then one summer day, she called to see if she could stop by right then and there. In the middle of a workout on my treadmill, I told her that this wasn't the best time. Dripping with sweat, I asked if it could wait, since I needed a shower. But she pressed, "Please, Kristen. It's important."

Inferring from her tone that this must be some kind of emergency, I told her, "Of course, you're welcome to come right over."

A few minutes later, the doorbell rang, and she came inside, where I directed her to my sofa. Getting to the point lickety-split, she said, "Kristen, why are you never available? It really hurts my feelings the way you brush off getting together with me. It makes me feel like I'm not a priority."

I took a deep breath, hoping I didn't look as annoyed as I felt. *Who does she think she is coming in here and demanding I spend time with her? Who is she to boss me and dictate to me what is and isn't a priority?* I thought to myself.

And then another thought shot down from heaven and turned down the heat on my internal pot of water billowing past the boiling point: *Well, Kristen, now you know exactly what Aundrea felt all those years ago. The question is, How will you respond now that you're on the other side of the fence?*

Thanks to a good dose of the Holy Spirit, I realized I needed to show compassion while also making clear the confines of what I could do.

I told her, "I'm so, so sorry I've hurt your feelings. Please know I'd never intentionally do that, although as I said, I'm sorry to have done it just the same. Also know that it's true that

I simply don't have the time available to get together that you'd like. Quite honestly, I think you expect more from this friendship than I'm able to give."

And then I let the silence hang while she stared at me.

I don't remember what she said after that, but I do remember that our friendship didn't bounce back afterward. On the one hand, I was honestly relieved to have breathing room out from under her many expectations. On the other, I hated contributing to another person's loneliness.

Alas, sometimes making a hard choice—like gently but firmly explaining how someone's expectations are affecting us— is the right thing to do, come what may.

Another way we avoid placing expectations on others is to spend time with God every day. As a Christian and believer in Jesus, I can tell you that my regular time with the Lord means I let God, the One whose bandwidth for us is limitless and can't be exhausted, fill me up. Meeting with Him every day by way of reading from the Bible, and perhaps a devotional too, means I'm plugged into the One who has infinite capacity for my needs. Doing this means I also feel readier to face the day in a hundred different ways.

What's more, it stops me from placing unreasonable expectations on my friends—not to mention my husband, children, and other loved ones. C. S. Lewis wrote,

When I have learnt to love God better than my earthly dearest, I shall love my earthly dearest better than I do now. In so far as I learn to love my earthly dearest at the expense of God and instead of God, I shall be moving towards the state in which I shall not love my earthly dearest at all. When first things are put first, second things are not suppressed but increased.[3]

Put time with the Lord first and feel the satisfaction of your "second things," like earthly friendships, placed in proper perspective. When time with God is our priority and we learn to receive His love first instead of demanding it from people, we don't burden them. We bless them. From the abundance He gives, we learn to genuinely extend His love to others. In that healthy soil, our friendships bloom and grow. This means the "second things" so often take care of themselves as we engage with people from a satisfied, thankful place.

While I'm never a perfect friend (none of us are!), putting first things first helps me be a good one.

What's more, while expectations may kill friendships, kindness in the form of low-stakes overtures feeds them. Reaching out with a chill attitude rather than a desperate demeanor goes a long way to good results. This is the difference in asking if your friend, or your potential new friend, can meet for coffee once instead of asking her to commit to a weekly coffee date. Of course, your first coffee date could turn into weekly or monthly get-togethers. The truth is that if God means for that person to be your friend, He will move her heart to want the same timeframe. Not only that, He'll move her heart to reciprocate your overtures with her own.

For easy reference, here's a quick list of ways that expectations can strangle the life right out of a friendship:

- Making demands on her time
- Asking for explanations about her schedule
- "Communication-bombing" her—exhibiting a pattern of frequent communication via several outlets in quick succession (DMs, texts, Snaps)
- Chronic oversharing and getting upset when she doesn't respond or reciprocate

- Digitally checking her comments or Snapchat scores to compare her communication with others to her communication with you
- Getting annoyed or angry when she spends time with other friends
- Jockeying for invitations
- Being easily offended
- Engaging in controlling or manipulating behaviors
- Gossiping

Instead, we can imitate behaviors like these that give life to our friendships:

- Doing the opposite of everything I just listed
- Giving the benefit of the doubt
- Listening well and asking follow-up questions about what she shares
- Pitching out several day and time options for getting together for coffee or lunch
- And if none of those work, asking if you can check in with her later when her schedule eases up
- Looking for opportunities to serve her with no strings attached (helping out when she or someone in her family is sick; offering to make her dinner and bring it over)
- Offering to pick up a few groceries for her from the store
- Finding out when her birthday is and treating her in some small way
- Passing along a book you enjoyed because you think she'll love it too

Scripture tells us, "Help and give without expecting a return. You'll never—I promise—regret it. Live out this God-created identity the way our Father lives toward us, generously and graciously, even when we're at our worst. Our Father is kind; you be kind" (Luke 6:35 MSG).

We give to give; we don't give to get. We give with no expectations in return. In obedience we move kindly in a friendship as the Holy Spirit directs. And we pray the Holy Spirit will move the heart of the other person to want to reciprocate. But if they don't, we don't demand it, and we don't internalize it negatively. We allow them to move onward in freedom. We can't force a friendship to look the way we want it to. If the connection doesn't happen, that's our cue to give our time and attention to other friends or potential friends—those people who *want* to travel in our lane.

And for those who don't, we simply wave as we pass them by.

HOW TO BE A GOOD FRIEND TO OTHERS

Subtle and overt expectations can end a friendship. If you want to be a good friend, you have to keep unreasonable expectations out of the relationship. Instead of placing unreasonable expectations on a friend, offer her kindness by way of simple, laid-back overtures. Whatever the state of your friendship, the least committed friend is the one who holds the map for where the friendship is going.

CHAPTER 10

PIONEER UP

Whenever there is doubt—don't.
OSWALD CHAMBERS, *MY UTMOST FOR HIS HIGHEST*

When I released my book *Back Roads to Belonging*, I had the opportunity to be on Annie F. Downs's *That Sounds Fun* podcast. Annie used to write for the website (in)courage alongside me, so I've known her for several years, well before my scheduled interview with her. I adore Annie, who lives in Nashville, and I love to hear her talk about everything from theology to country music. Known for her mega-fun demeanor and megawatt personality, Annie quickly settled right into a comfortable conversation with me during the podcast interview.

At one point, our discussion turned to how I met my husband. As the story goes, David and I, after making eyes at each other as we crossed paths in the Oklahoma State orchestra, found ourselves in the same stairwell of the music building one afternoon. Headed in opposite directions, we both paused and proceeded to talk and talk and *talk* for an hour and a half. Not only did I like what I saw in David Strong; I liked what I heard too. Unlike a lot of college fellas, he was down-to-earth and confident without the cocky. While our stairwell conversation revealed a sizable age gap between us, our dialogue flowed naturally and effortlessly.

Age gap or not, yours truly was smitten.

Eventually, we both had classes to attend, so we said our goodbyes before heading in our own directions. I was optimistic that David dug my action as I did his, so before I walked upstairs, I said rather breezily, "Hey . . . would you like to exchange phone numbers?"

David's response? "Ummm, no . . . that's okay."

And that's when my cloud-nine, breezy self promptly plummeted to earth with the thought, *Whatever, college boy. WHAT-E-VER.*

As I explained to Annie in the interview, David had partly refused to exchange numbers because he wondered if I was too young to date. (I was eighteen and he was twenty-six.) Fair point.[1] However, what he didn't mention to me until later was that he refused my number because he already had it. For some inexplicable reason, he didn't think to share that fact with me in the moment. *Shrugs shoulders.*

With his sister's encouragement (thanks, Kathy!), David gave me a call and asked me out a week or so later. On February 15, 1993, we had our first date, and we've been together ever since.

After hearing this part of the story, Annie asked, "Can you remember back to what you were you thinking that week between when y'all talked for an hour and a half in the stairwell and when he finally asked you out?"

I told her that while I thought about him and hoped that I'd get to have another conversation with him, I only gave a small amount of mental real estate to thinking about him and wondering what might (or might not) happen next. I had classes and rehearsals and all kinds of college-y things that filled my time, so I largely went about my business and did what needed to be done.

Reflecting on this, Annie said, "You just had to wait."

"Yes, exactly. I had to wait to see what would happen—if anything would happen at all."

She followed that with, "It's one of the problems we do have now: You don't have to wait. It's uncommon that someone doesn't have social media, so women have to think differently."[2]

She was right: Because of social media, no one has to wait to see a glimpse of what someone else is doing when that person isn't communicating with them.

In today's world, if someone is slow to return a message or touch base with us, we can essentially spy on them to see what they're doing. Or we can "nudge" them to respond by checking in with them instead of sitting back and waiting to see what might happen—which was largely people's only course of action until a couple of decades ago.

Annie went on to share a story about a conversation she had with a friend who was in a potential relationship with a fellow, but her friend didn't know what he was going to do next regarding her. Would he reach out or not? Annie told her friend, "Just pretend it's 1850, and there's nothing you can do. Just wait and give him a little time. Pretend you can't follow him on Instagram. Pretend you can't text him."

We both laughed after I responded to her story with two simple words: "Pioneer up!"

Yes. Because whether we're talking about dating relationships or friendships, it's well and good at times for us to act like it's 1850 and pioneer up. That is, to act like we're without social media and have no way to spy on others or fret about them or attempt to force a response from someone. I *know* this is much easier said than done. You may even believe it is completely unreasonable for this day and age! I get that; I truly do. But it seems like a healthier alternative to driving ourselves crazy by digitally spying on someone.

Let's say you've gone walking around your neighborhood with a potential friend, and you really like her and hope you two become better pals. Maybe you'd even like to schedule another time for you both to grab a bite to eat or go to a movie together. So you reach out to her via text or direct message to get another date on the calendar. An hour or an afternoon or a whole day goes by, and you don't hear anything in response. To make matters worse, you can see that she read your message. You start to sense that low-level panic that tells you, *She's ignoring your message because she doesn't want to get together again.*

This is when it's time to pioneer up and behave as if you don't have so many ways to immediately communicate. We pioneer up and remember that people have many priorities in their lives, and we don't fault them for taking care of those priorities. Many of us living in the Western world are addicted to immediacy, and one way this plays out is internally going off the rails when someone doesn't respond to our communication as quickly as we think they should. So we pioneer up because it gives ourselves *and* the other person some breathing room to be about our busy lives.

It can often be a short trip from someone not responding in a timely manner to our thinking, *I guess she got to know me more and didn't like what she saw. I wonder what's wrong with me that makes her not want to get together with me again.*

Pioneering up helps us stay off that dead-end road. We do it because it gives us a way to redirect our thoughts to healthier, friendlier territory.

Of course, we don't pioneer up as an alternative to accepting reality. We do it because the truth is, the people we communicate with *do* have busy lives that make it hard to respond to every message immediately. We want to cut them the slack we'd like to receive ourselves when our own lives get in the way of responding to communication quickly—or when simple explanations occur, like that her phone died shortly after she read the message.

The fact is that for the other person, your message and my message may fall under the "it can wait" category. Not because it's not important but because it's less important compared to the tasks her boss requested or the grocery shopping her family needs or the book she's reading on a rare quiet afternoon.

Or, because she's tending to all of this and more, she simply forgot to respond.

This is a hard thing for a Gen Xer like me to remember, yet I think it's even harder for the younger folks. If there's any group that has grown up with the privilege of "instant"—be that in consuming information or in communicating with others—it's the Gen Zers and younger, also dubbed the "digital natives" of today's culture. If you're Gen Z, perhaps you're familiar with this idea that if someone doesn't respond immediately to a particular Snap or Instagram DM or text, it's perceived as a negative. If so, you're not alone, as on some level, most of us entertain this thought, whatever our age! And while studies show Gen Z folks greatly value face-to-face connection, they also struggle with interpersonal skills as social media muddies the waters between friendships and acquaintances.[3] Casual connections are easily made, but deep, abiding friendships are more elusive.

I mention all this to say that while I'm well aware of the benefits of digital communication for *all* of us these days (heck, it helps me regularly chat with my three adult kids *and* earn a living!), there's never been a more ideal time to pioneer up.

Not only would employing this mindset help us manage the low-level anxiety that comes with slow responses in communication, but it could eventually help us swivel our energies toward relearning the value of face-to-face communication as we more readily practice the verbal and nonverbal cues of interpersonal communication.

While it's well and good to extend an invitation to someone, be a friend to the other person and keep a relaxed, low-stakes attitude over her response. From Instagram to Facebook, X/Twitter, Snapchat, TikTok, BeReal, texting, and email, there's eleventy gazillion ways of checking in with someone or following them around digitally in hopes of trying to alleviate our worries. Resist the urge to obsessively check All the Things in All the Places because, in the end, it usually stokes our fears rather than staves them off. Give others the freedom to live their lives, and give yourself the blessing of getting on with yours.

This begs another question: If we've been wise to pioneer up by exercising our freedom to not follow people around digitally, what is an appropriate amount of time to reenter the twenty-first century and touch base with someone who *hasn't* gotten back to us?

For me, the dividing line is in wanting to genuinely touch base with the person and not pester her. If I've asked a friend for coffee the following week and don't hear back from her, I'm not going to reach out and ask her about it again until a couple of days before the date I originally proposed coffee. I'm going to respond to her judiciously, not annoyingly. And if she still doesn't respond in return, well, I have a choice: I can roll with it or I can double down and get all up in her business by blowing up her phone. As off-putting as this is, I've been guilty of doing it to a degree. But all it does is scream, "PAY ATTENTION TO ME!" It makes the person receiving the battering of communication want to distance herself all the more. No one likes being literally or digitally controlled or pushed around.

Having said all this, let me point out the obvious fact that even as we're working hard to give others the benefit of the doubt, it's always possible that the other person doesn't reciprocate the desire to get to know us better. Sometimes our suspicions and fears about a message that remains on "read receipt" are confirmed. Our query or message never gets answered, and we may never know why. In those cases, we can still reach out again with a reminder. Sometimes, however, the reality is that the connection we felt with the potential friend goes only one direction. To recall the last chapter, we're not in the same lane. We must make peace with that, which means we don't internalize it as something being wrong with us, but rather that the connection wasn't meant to be. For whatever reason, her interest or circumstances changed, so a regularly practiced friendship with us is not a possibility in her current season.

It just means it's not the right friendship for us.

As I've said before, rejection isn't fun—don't I know it! In the context of friendships, rejection can be overwhelmingly painful, and I'll never minimize that. But it happens. By all means, take the time you need to mourn the loss of a beloved friend who back-burnered you. But don't let the pain from it run rampant and start to negatively boss your behavior. Talk about it with your mama or sister or counselor. Consider this passage from the Psalms; you have the most exuberant invitation to talk about it with God:

> You've always given me breathing room,
>   a place to get away from it all,
> A lifetime pass to your safe-house,
>   an open invitation as your guest.

You've always taken me seriously, God,
made me welcome among those who know and
love you. (Psalm 61:3–5 MSG)

What a life-giving thought that God takes all our concerns seriously—and that certainly includes our friendship concerns. There's no such thing as blowing up God's phone or being too needy for Him or too desperate for time with Him. Not only does He not mind our neediness and desperation, but He truly wants every last drop of them. He has tremendous compassion for the needy (Psalm 72:13). Because of His true-blue, all-in love for us, He's never too busy to talk with us. He never has something else He'd rather do than spend time with us. And when we spend time with Him, He fills us up. One beneficial byproduct of this is that we're not trying within an inch of our lives to get filled up by others. Instead, we're satisfied in His breathing room. In turn, we give that breathing room to others.

I didn't live during the pioneer days, but I did live in the latter 1900s when the inherent lack of urgency meant there was more grace for the fact that we all had lives we were living. And while people, including me, still forgot or ignored messages, we didn't slide so quickly into the realm where a lack of response was a negative reflection on us. Oh, I know we could still arrive there after a longer period of time. But there was much less potential for it to happen as frequently as it does today.

The actual pioneers had to constantly sew and mend clothing, stoke the fires for heat, grow their own vegetables, bake their bread, live through viral influenza, and find animals to hunt and kill for dinner. They didn't have time to worry too much about a plethora of people's motives for communication, or lack thereof. While most of us are not spending our days with those exact to-dos, we have other things going on that prevent us from reaching out or responding to people immediately. Whether a two-way friendship connection following spotty communication is there or not, let's relax instead of reacting.

Give yourself and others grace by pioneering up.

HOW TO BE A GOOD FRIEND TO OTHERS

A "pioneer up" mindset helps us keep a breezy attitude toward communication with potential friends because it discourages us from fretting about or trying to force a response from someone. Be a good friend to others by relaxing rather than reacting when someone doesn't communicate with you as quickly as you think she should. Give people room to live their busy, multifaceted lives, and you'll find you have more time and ability to do the same—no matter which way the friendship goes.

CHAPTER 11

TELL PEOPLE WHAT YOU THINK OF THEM (NO, REALLY)

*Language is how you give intention to your
intuition and how you share your vision with
others. Language is how you create a culture.*
WILL GUIDARA, *UNREASONABLE HOSPITALITY*

A s a kid, my younger sister, Sara, was an excellent softball
pitcher and all-around player. One day, as her team prepared to take the field before a game, I sat in the stands
watching Sara warm up on the pitcher's mound.

While enjoying my Fun Dip candy, I heard a girl directly
behind me say, "*Gah*. Sara pitches *sooo* slow. It's a wonder the ball
even gets over the plate."

My eyes narrowed as I leaned back ever so slightly, placing
my Fun Dip stick in its packet of cherry-flavored sugar.

Now, Sara would be the first to tell you that she wasn't the fastest softball pitcher in the league. However, she had incredible accuracy regarding the strike zone. The girl sitting behind me was a pitcher too, and she pitched fast, yes. But she also pitched wild and loose—kind of like her tongue in that moment. I'd witnessed her unpredictable pitches whack batters on knees, hips, shoulders, and elsewhere. Because of her savage, inconsistent pitching, I also witnessed a lot of hitters shake like leaves while standing in the batter's box.

I continued to listen to this girl—whose name I know but won't share to protect the not-so-innocent—make fun of Sara's pitching. Finally, I stood up, whirled around, and said very pointedly, "Well, unlike *you*, Sara knows where the strike zone is *and* how to pitch a ball straight through it!"

I don't remember what she said after that, but I know the comments about my sister stopped posthaste.

By and large, I'm not one for confrontation, especially with people who have no influence on my day-to-day life. And you could argue that God wasn't necessarily pleased with twelve-year-old me insulting this girl as I told her off. But this is still true today: If I hear someone badmouth my sister or my sister-friends, I don't mind setting that person straight.

Not only do I refuse to tolerate people who talk ugly about my friends; I want to speak affectionately about my friends whether they're in the room or not. I want to speak affectionately *to* my friends.

In a University of Utah study, college freshmen were asked to keep a record of activities done with new friends. After three months' time, the study showed that close friendships were more likely to form when both parties expressed affection for each other.[1] So herein lies a concrete course of action we can take to build up and strengthen our friendships: With warmth and kindheartedness, tell your friends what you think of them.

I realize that if making friends is awkward, offering small gestures of affection can feel awkward too. Worse still, it can feel disingenuous, like you're just trying to butter someone up by giving a compliment so you can receive one in return.

However, offering someone affection through a verbal or written compliment or praise won't feel or appear disingenuous if you mean it. The motive of your heart behind what you say or do is what makes the difference. Also, the more you make this a habit, the more natural it will feel to express.

Perhaps you're thinking that encouraging your friends is a darling notion . . . *if* you have friends. If you don't, you may ask, "Where are all these people I'm supposed to go up to and start telling they have well-behaved kids—or even better—that I can sympathize when their kids aren't well behaved?"

Back when I was in college in Ohio and having a hard time making friends, I learned that a simple, genuine compliment to someone else may not turn an exchange into a friendship, but it could lead to someone blooming a bit. So if I saw someone, whether an acquaintance or a stranger, wearing something cute or handling something well, I would tell them.

And here's the thing: We often *think* kind words about others, but we're not always so adept at *saying* them. When those thoughts come to us, whether it's about a friend we've known for a decade or someone we just met in line at Torchy's Tacos, we can get into the practice of saying them out loud.

When Maria showed up in my Sunday school class a few years ago, the first thing I noticed about her was that the color she wore (kelly green) looked really good on her. I told her it did, too, as I introduced myself. At that time, I wasn't necessarily looking for a new friend. And yet, God knew I needed the friendship found in one Maria of Colorado Springs.

After one conversation with Maria, I witnessed how she

spent affection like she had a millionaire's budget for it. She listened in a way that let you know she was interested in what you were saying. She gave attention like the person she spoke with was the only one in the room. She enveloped the other person with kindness, warmth, and affection, and she still does.

So how does Maria do that, exactly? Well, in a few different ways. She won't let your conversation with her end without encouraging you in some way—like telling you how sorry she is for what you're going through. Or maybe she'll mention how, all things considered, you're handling that challenge well. Or she'll tell you what her own experience has been in a similar circumstance.

Also, she's a master at seeing and naming good qualities in whomever she's around.

Some things I've heard her say to people include,

"Oh, I love your style!"
"You're so funny!"
"You're such a good mom!"
"Well done, you!"
"You sure love your people well."
"What's the hardest thing about working from home/
     homeschooling your kids/caring for a disabled
     loved one?"
"Can I have the recipe for the Lemony Chicken and Potato
     Soup you made? It was delicious!"[2]

Maria doesn't only tell people what she thinks of them in the best kinds of ways. She *shows* them what she thinks of them too. If you ask her to pray for your kids, she'll proceed to pray for them like they're her own. If she reads something that reminds her of you, she'll take the time to send it to you as personal encouragement. She's generous to cry *with* you. And she'll holler from the top of Pikes Peak in celebration over your successes.

Maria isn't loud or dramatic; she's not "extra," as the kids say. In her own quiet manner, she confidently comforts and encourages in a way that satisfies a weary spirit. No matter how dissonant your day was, her words have a way of helping you end on a tonic note.

Maria is a spectacular friend—a total hype girl. But she would be the first to tell you that she doesn't have a spectacularly complicated way of befriending women. Maria does a hundred small gestures consistently, and that leads to consistent friendships.

I'd bet that Maria would also tell you I'm being too generous with my assessment of her, and that would be her honest take of it, not a humblebrag. What's more, Maria would tell you that she hasn't always been the affectionate grace-giver she is now.

One day, after witnessing Maria respond patiently with someone who, in my opinion, had behaved rudely and elicited a covert eye roll from me, I asked her point-blank, "Maria, what causes you to have an endless source of grace and kindness with people?"

She responded that she'd been rather "judgy" till she met a friend, Jen, as a camp counselor decades earlier. At this camp, Jen worked alongside Maria on kitchen cleanup. This camp hosted a lot of kids from wealthy families, and Maria witnessed a lot of those kids behaving in a rude, entitled way. But she also witnessed Jen repeatedly look for what good each person offered, and then Jen would say a kind word about that.

From that point onward, Maria saw the world through different eyes. She said, "I remember, too, that God loves me, and because of the grace He's shown me, I can show grace to others.

Also, most people—if not all—have a backstory of pain, and I want to be one who eases that pain, not adds to it."

That's not to say that Maria doesn't have a backbone. I've witnessed her judiciously correct negative talk and stand up to bad behavior. But I love this idea that a friend of hers from long ago influenced the way she behaves as a friend today. And that in turn influences the way I and others behave as affectionate, grace-filled friends.

Contrast this to watching one wilt when the opposite happens. I recall a time when my friend Aimée saw me flinch after she overheard another friend of mine make a snide comment about my cooking. After the incident, Aimée said, "What was the point of her criticizing you like that? And besides, you're a great cook!"

Regarding that person, I'd become so accustomed to her pinpricks of negative comments that while I felt them, I assumed no one else noticed them. So I was genuinely surprised that Aimée had.

I said to her, "Oh, you noticed that?"

She responded, "Heck yeah, I did. It was completely unnecessary."

Aimée is perceptive, and her observation woke me up to the fact that this friend's behavior brought harm, if only little by little. But death by a thousand paper cuts still ain't a fun way to go. And until Aimée named the poor behavior for what it was—rude and unnecessary—I didn't realize how negatively it affected me. It repelled me from that friend rather than drawing me toward her.

Will Guidara, the former owner of the New York City four-star restaurant Eleven Madison Park, says this in his book *Unreasonable Hospitality*: "Whether criticism or praise, it's a leader's job to give their team feedback *all the time*. But every person on the team should be hearing more about what they did well than what they could do better, or they're going to feel deflated and unmotivated."[3]

Of course, Will's talking about praise and constructive criticism, not the kind of critical comments my friend had been throwing my way. But the same principle works in forming friendships as it does in leading teams: If you want to build and nurture good friendships, your friends need to receive praise, and they certainly need to hear it more than your criticism.

While it's always good to learn about our own behavioral blind spots, it's also good to evaluate blind spots we may have regarding another's behavior—toward us and others. If that behavior is regularly leaving us deflated and unmotivated, it's okay to limit our contact with that person.

The Bible also tells us to keep affection in our lexicon of positive behaviors:

> Make every effort to add to your faith goodness; and to goodness, knowledge; and to knowledge, self-control; and to self-control, perseverance; and to perseverance, godliness; and to godliness, mutual affection; and to mutual affection, love. For if you possess these qualities in increasing measure, they will keep you from being ineffective and unproductive in your knowledge of our Lord Jesus Christ. (2 Peter 1:5–8)

When we add mutual affection and, consequently, love to the equation of our interactions, we remain effective and productive as we experience more of what Jesus has for us. And since we know Jesus wants us to have our true-blue friends, we know that intentionally sharing affection with others (and not hoarding it) is one way to strengthen those bonds of comradery.

Maria spends affection by telling people what she thinks of

them, in part, because she acts from the overflow of grace Jesus spent on her behalf. This is true, and yet it's also true that she radiates the love of Jesus. Dr. Timothy Keller stated, "People who have a strong friendship with God have a poise and a peace that makes them attractive to others."[4] This is a big reason Maria's friends are drawn to her. She's not only as warm and comforting as a cozy fire; she also has a very clear love for Jesus that makes a friendship with her appealing.

What's more, this reminds me that a great place to work on my friendships is to work on my friendship with Jesus first so that I have that Light-drenched quality that draws others toward me.

Maria was initially a surprise friend who eventually became one of my most treasured. But she puts in the work to be that way with me and others.

A friend of mine who spent several years as the codirector of a preschool told me that one of her schools had a "words of affirmation" board with seasonal cutouts. For example, in the fall, the cutouts would be leaf-shaped, and staff members were encouraged to pick out a leaf or two and write words of affirmation on them about other staff members.

Inevitably, according to my friend, some people weren't interested in writing words of affirmation to each other, and yet those same people would complain that no one wrote words of affirmation about them.

In other words, they wanted others to put in the work that they themselves weren't willing to put in toward others.

And aren't we all like those staff members from time to time? Even though we know better, we want the benefits of friendship without the work. And sometimes that "work" looks like noticing what others are doing around us and encouraging them in some way based on what we see.

Yes, it may initially feel awkward to name the good you see

in another, but it gets easier with practice. Perhaps you do it verbally, perhaps in the old-timey, written way or via a text. In our connected but lonely times, these actions can turn "a fleeting moment into a tangible, beautiful gift—one that is sent off to be cherished."[5]

Through words written or spoken and small actions taken, affectionately telling people what you think of them can elongate your presence in another's life and strengthen the bonds of connection . . . thereby fortifying the friendship.

Will Guidara also writes, "Let your energy impact the people you're talking to, as opposed to the other way around."[6] When you go into an environment bent on telling people what you think of them in a loving way, you'll be doing exactly that.

HOW TO BE A GOOD FRIEND TO OTHERS

Noticing and naming the good you see in and around other women encourages and builds them up—and your friendships with them. Practice this on acquaintances and strangers and watch them bloom! Your energy will positively impact them as it grows your friendships.

CHAPTER 12

FREUDENFREUDE IS YOUR
RELATIONAL SUPERPOWER

*Jo's eyes sparkled, for it is always pleasant to
be believed in; and a friend's praise is always
sweeter than a dozen newspaper puffs.*
LOUISA MAY ALCOTT, *LITTLE WOMEN*

For nearly fifteen years now, I've been a staff writer for
(in)courage, the online community of DaySpring, which is
a subsidiary of Hallmark Cards. Roughly thirty (in)courage
staff writers share personal stories at any given time to connect
women to God and one another.

From its beginning in 2009, writers have come and gone, but
no matter how the group changes, one thing stays consistent: the
way its team members cheer for one another. While we live in
many places inside and outside of the United States, we're fiercely

united in celebrating each member's success. So when one person signs a book deal or receives a much-wanted answer to prayer, they can feel the joy in the messages as we celebrate corporately. The writing team beautifully embodies what I learned is called *freudenfreude*. Also, it's beautifully reflected in our community at large, as the comments to our articles prove over and over again.

I happened upon this word recently, and I wholeheartedly delighted in it. *Freudenfreude*, inspired by the German word for joy, can be defined as "the bliss we feel when someone else succeeds, even if we weren't directly involved."[1]

Perhaps you're thinking this could've been a part of the last chapter. After all, I did mention how telling others what you think of them in a good way or sharing affection can look like rejoicing in another's success. But I wanted it to have its own chapter because when friends exercise *freudenfreude* for each other, they activate a relational superpower. Unlike anything else, it benefits and builds up friendships. What's more, it benefits and builds up our own mental health in the process.

If you want to find your people, engaging in *freudenfreude* will draw folks to you like bees to honey.

Still, sometimes putting this into practice is difficult. Rejoicing over another's success can taste like vinegar going down—especially if it's a success we'd like to have ourselves.

My dream of writing books began in the heart of my ten-year-old self. And when I finally dusted off that dream and began actively pursuing it by putting together a book proposal at thirty-six or thirty-seven years old, I had someone tell me, "Don't get your hopes up on that working out." (Honestly, several people told me some version of that, and admittedly, for good reason.) Later, when I told that same person about how I'd signed with a publisher to write my first book, I watched as she said

"Congratulations" with her words but said the opposite with her face and body language.

I knew in that moment exactly how she felt: no congratulatory bliss over my success. And I bet you don't have to reach far back in your memory to think of someone who felt no bliss over various successes of your own. Perhaps you can even think of someone who displayed *schadenfreude*, which is defined as the "pleasure felt when witnessing someone's misfortune."[2]

Schadenfreude is the opposite of *freudenfreude*.

To be fair, most of us have taken pleasure in someone's misfortune. Studies show that while giving in to a little *schadenfreude* is normal (like I do when my college rival, the OU Sooners, lose a football game), indulging in that too often lowers a person's self-esteem.[3]

One of the unhappiest folks I've ever met told me years ago about how she regularly followed a website designed around slamming a particular A-list actress. I remember thinking, *Why in the world would you spend time and energy creating a slanderous website? And for the love of all that's holy, why read such garbage?*

But of course, people do just that to the A-list actresses, as well as to the awkward middle school kid whose mean-spirited peers would rather make fun of than get to know. Make no mistake: Trolls come in all shapes and sizes, and they seem to have all kinds of time to cowardly slander those in the arena rather than contribute something worthwhile. But clearly, whether you're a creator or consumer of that kind of nonsense, engaging in that activity screams, "I AM NOT A HAPPY, FULFILLED PERSON."

I don't troll people or read their defamatory material; I put a boundary as wide as the Mississippi between myself and that kind of conduct (and between myself and others who engage in that kind of conduct). But before I get too far down the road on my high horse, I'll confess I'm still guilty of acting out of insecurities toward others, like refusing to celebrate their successes.

When I was in eighth grade, a girl in my class won an award that I'd *desperately* hoped to get. When I heard that she'd received the award, I didn't rejoice in her success. Instead, I responded with a catty and rude, "Well, the cream always rises to the top, so *I'll* get it next time." My friend Heather, who sat next to me, heard the comment and immediately hollered in horror, "KRISTEN!!" I sincerely apologized to the girl receiving the award, for as soon as I said what I said, I felt a stabbing pang of conviction that could only have come from heaven. I knew good and well that I'd behaved mean as a snake, and I regretted it. *But* I held on to the disappointment and inner entitlement I felt.

No wonder indulging in a great deal of *schadenfreude* lowers a person's self-esteem.[4] Contrast that to *freudenfreude*: "Sharing in someone else's joy can also foster resilience, improve life satisfaction, and help people cooperate during conflict."[5] What's more, it's a kind of social glue that makes relationships "more intimate and enjoyable."[6]

Author Kari Kampakis says, "Maybe if we quit taking our insecurities out on each other, we can love each other properly."[7] *Freudenfreude* is a natural outpouring of this, in which we default to encouraging and building up one another rather than taking pleasure in another's misfortune because of our own insecurities.

Does grown-up Kristen still sometimes wish I could have another's blessing, whatever that is? I do. Comparison is an enemy that masquerades as a friend telling you what you "deserve," and sometimes it's hard to shake her pushy presence from you.

But giving the very thing she tries to take from us—our humility, gratitude, and joy for another's gifts and giftings—is how we up the *freudenfreude* factor in our friendships. Feeling negatively about another's successes is neither here nor there. Being a grown-up is not acting strictly according to how we feel but acting according to what's right. It's calling ourselves to higher and better. I don't give a bleepity-bleep about how we feel about it. There's no excuse for acting ugly and rude toward another person, especially toward her good news.

If we're feeling resentful or negative in some way toward another's accomplishments, it's best to take that to Jesus and pray for Him to change our hearts. And while we wait for that to happen, we look at the other person, smile, and say, "Well done!" or "That's wonderful!" or "Congratulations!"

In situations like this, we do the right thing and then wait for our feelings to catch up. More often than not, they will.

If this is hard for you, it helps to keep in mind the big-picture view: God isn't pulling all our "wins" from one giant pool, where one person's gain means the rest of us are left with less. What another person accomplishes does nothing to blight the blessings God has in store for you. Don't sacrifice your integrity to have your say, like I did in eighth grade.

Instead, magnify your integrity by cheering for others. Luke 6:38 says, "Give, and it will be given to you. A good measure, pressed down, shaken together and running over, will be poured into your lap. For with the measure you use, it will be measured to you."

Give *freudenfreude* generously to others and get friendship, among other things, in return.

So what are some practical ways we can up the *freudenfreude* factor in our friendships? We can exercise *freudenfreude* every time we pray for another's success. When our prayers for others are answered as we hoped, we share in giving God the glory. And when they're not, we can still provide a hopeful perspective about our friend's future.

Also, consider asking your friends and potential friends questions such as these to foster a spirit of *freudenfreude*:

- "What's the best thing that's happened to you recently?"
- "What's one dream you'd like to see fulfilled?"
- "What's one thing you believe you're good at doing?"
- "Who's one person in your life who has positively influenced you and why?"

Or, it could be as simple as noticing a small or big success about the other person and responding accordingly:

- "Gosh, I love your sweater! May I ask where you found that?"
- "That dessert you made for the reception was so good. May I have the recipe?"
- "I saw the way you handled your kids' outburst—good job, mama!"
- "I overheard the way that lady spoke to you, and I applaud your ability to be gracious in return."

Then listen for her answers and respond positively to what she says. I know from personal experience that doing so goes a long way to improve the friendship's fitness by becoming a multi-vitamin for it.

I've learned firsthand how practicing *freudenfreude* not only celebrates the one I'm talking with but also helps her joy become my own as it bubbles up and over effervescently. We grow our own joy, a fruit of the Spirit (Galatians 5:22–23), when we join in celebrating other people's joy. Their joy becomes our own because at the end of the day, success for our friends is success for us too.

At this point in my life, I've learned that celebrating my friends' and loved ones' achievements feels dang good. God rewards goodwill with good feelings.

As with other principles discussed in this book, practicing *freudenfreude* helps us become more proficient at it. We can rejoice in a friend's success, and it takes not one iota from myself or my own successes.

And celebrating our friends' successes increases the likelihood of successful friendships—something we all can feel good about.

HOW TO BE A GOOD FRIEND TO OTHERS

Freudenfreude is a relational superpower. Expressing your joy over another's success will help you enjoy more successful friendships!

CHAPTER 13

THE BENEFITS OF BOOKEND FRIENDS

*Are our spiritual eyes wide open as
we look for our people? Or are we so
programmed with a "same age, same stage"
mentality that we're missing the women
who are ahead of us and behind us?*
SOPHIE HUDSON, *GIDDY UP, EUNICE*

It's easy for me to know I need peers who are my age and within my own life stage, but I don't always think about intentionally finding those a life stage or two ahead of or behind me.

It can be tempting to believe our friends need to look and act a certain way to be worth our time and investment. They should be single if we're single, have kids if we have kids. They need to be Protestant if we're Protestant, Catholic if we're Catholic.

They need to be happier when a certain someone sits in the Oval Office, just like we are.

There's not a thing wrong with having same-stage friends who, for example, understand the way a toddler or a teen throws a fit over the word *no*. But when we're wanting friends, we also need to enlarge our field of vision for where we look for them.

When we lived for the second time in Dayton, Ohio, I joined a Bible study at my family's church, Emmanuel Lutheran. I invited Louise, the darling newlywed wife of a good family friend, to join the study with me. Most of the ladies in the study were three or four life stages ahead of us. This made Louise the baby and me the preschooler compared to the mostly Empty Nester group of gals.

The Bible study met on Wednesday mornings while my twin sons were in the church's preschool program. After dropping James and Ethan off at their classroom in the church basement, I'd drop off my baby girl, Faith, at the childcare room. For most of my Bible studies with those ladies, Faith was the only child in childcare. I still can't believe my church offered childcare for my one single wee-watt, but that's exactly what it did. And gosh, did I ever relish that golden time with the grown-up ladies.

Our pastor's wife, Deb, led all our studies, which were usually penned by a dynamic blonde named Beth Moore. Deb would begin our time with prayer, and then we'd discuss anything about the Bible study homework that inspired us. Often, what stood out to us in the teaching would lead to discussions about how we were applying what we learned in our own lives. Then we'd watch the study's accompanying video and reflect together on the teaching. Before we parted for the week, Deb would ask for prayer requests.

I don't know about you, but I often dread the out-loud requests for prayers—especially when I'm new to a particular group. That is, I find it rather awkward to share my own personal prayer requests with a new group of gals I've known for ten minutes. I don't mind listening to other people's one bit. But while listening to theirs, I'm spending no small amount of time weighing what prayer request I should share. I'm more likely to share a "lighter" one that skims the waters of vulnerability but doesn't dive headlong into them. After all, "the righteous choose their friends carefully" (Proverbs 12:26).

While I may've remained a smidge guarded with those ladies at the beginning, it wasn't long before I took to them like a duck to water. So I felt safe to dive deeper. The general idea regularly expressed by those ladies from the get-go was that by their stage of life, they'd seen and experienced it all. There wasn't a pearl-clutcher in the bunch; it was impossible to shock them.

My faith exploded during those years, in part because if you throw yourself into Beth's studies, you can't help but be brought closer to Jesus. But it also exploded because of the way those ladies reflected the love of Jesus to me and for me. Each of them faced their own brand of struggles, yet they modeled life choices that kept a heavenly vision in mind. They perpetually looked up instead of out at their own troubles.

Between each of them and Beth Moore, I wanted the kind of faith that made them a collective delight.

When mid-November rolled around that first year, Deb announced that we wouldn't be meeting the Wednesday before Thanksgiving. I gasped and said dramatically, "*Noooooooooo! Can't we please still meet anyway?*"

Since most of the ladies were preparing food for a posse of people, the answer was a resounding no.

Just as these gals cooked for and loved on their own families, they cared for me like family even though we weren't related. Of course, I was profoundly loved by my beloved grandmas and great-aunts, but they all lived in Oklahoma. For the three years my family lived in Ohio, these local ladies loved me, led me, mentored me, and advised me. They, as well as Louise, were Jesus' ambassadors of affection within the walls of that room, loving me through their presence, perspectives, and prayers. Honest to goodness, I still reap rewards today from the ways they blessed me then. They were gushing fountains of wisdom, and I never missed a chance to soak up their smarts. They showed me the art of encouragement, and I don't think I'd be the encourager I am today without them.

What seeped into the nooks and crannies of that study were a thousand overtures of true-blue friendship. And to this day, when I think back to those years, I can't help but tear up over the tenderness of that time with Deb, Barb, Nell, Penny, Robin, and the others.

Relationships like these are often described as "intergenerational friendships." I also like to think of these ladies as my "bookend friends," people who are a life stage or two ahead of or behind me who help me stand tall in my present-day life.

Whether we're the ones being encouraged or doing the encouraging, we find there's a lot of friendship real estate to be explored in those a good deal older and younger than us.

Bookend Friends in Front of Us

Seasonal bookend friends further down the road from us give us a healthy perspective about where we are and what's to come. When it's too early for us to find encouraging, green growth within the fresh soil underneath our feet, these friends help us keep on keepin' on where we are today. They remind us that, as ones who've been where we are, growth takes time. What we see now isn't necessarily what lies in the future. The way things are now isn't the way they'll be forever. These friends help us see the "goodness of the LORD in the land of the living" (Psalm 27:13) when we're called to pick up stakes—and when we're called to stay put where we are.

The words and actions of these bookend friends become shade trees to rest under as well as sturdy bridges to cross over into the next stage of life. They equip you to be prepared and expectant for what is ahead as they remind you of what we ultimately want to know: All will be well.

These bookend friends have impacted me the most in the area of parenting. During those Bible study days, these women assured me that my daughter wouldn't be two forever, and her strong-willed personality would serve her well one day. They promised that if I stayed diligent with my son, who hated being bossed but sure loved to boss others, he would one day develop into a bang-up leader. They affirmed that my other son would outgrow his finickiness for everything from toothbrushes to scratchy tags in T-shirts.

They were correct on every count and proved that, indeed, "the heartfelt counsel of a friend is as sweet as perfume and incense" (Proverbs 27:9 NLT).

My friend Jamie is drawn to older friends because, in her words, it feels like she doesn't need to impress them. This resonates with me too. Sometimes a spirit of competition or jealousy can seep into a peer-to-peer friendship more readily than intergenerational ones. Because intergenerational friendships mean both parties are usually in different life stages, that competitiveness is left by the wayside. Plus, older women are so often hard to surprise or offend. The relief of that lets us automatically exhale and relax in their presence.

As I discovered with the Emmanuel Lutheran ladies, older

friends also hold storehouses of wisdom. There's a groundedness to them that serves as a solid place to rest our hearts.

Bookend Friends Behind Us

Seasonal bookend friends a little behind us are those we get to encourage by providing a healthy perspective on where they are and what's coming their way.

I recently asked this question to my people on Instagram: "How have intergenerational friendships rewarded you?" My favorite response was from Kim, who said, in a pithy fashion, that from older friends she receives wisdom; and from younger friends, she receives energy. I couldn't agree more! While the younger folks can certainly bring the wisdom, another reason I love to hang out with them is that they do bring an energy and vitality to my conversations and life.

While I love living in the forest on five acres as I have for the past nine years, I often miss our previous neighborhood, where we lived next door to the most darling young family with two small children. Neighborhoods with small children are chock-full of laughter and life. And while I don't miss the exhausting, in-the-trenches stage of life that is parenting tiny tots, there's no denying that brushing up to them brings me energy. (That is, until doing so depletes my energy!) And those of us with bookend friends behind us are in a position to help in a way that same-aged peers may not be able to replicate.

As much as I hope I encourage the bookend friends coming up behind me, several of my younger friends, like Louise, have been a constant source of encouragement for me. For example, more than once, I didn't believe I was handling a parenting problem very well, and Louise would suddenly say, "You're such a great mom!" While I looked at the day as a failure, she showed me a different picture.

Another younger friend of mine, Lindsey, is a delight to be around because not only does she encourage me where I am in my life today, but I also see where she is, knee-deep in the business of raising three fabulous middle school and high school sons, and I think, *Wow, I don't know if I appreciated all the hats I wore during those years, but as I watch someone else wear them, I sure can now.*

Also, while every person on the planet has wisdom to share through their personal experiences, Louise, Lindsey, and other younger friends of mine have done a lot to help me gain fresh perspectives that I wouldn't have considered otherwise.

Friends or Mentors?

Some may say, "Well, older women weren't so much friends to you, Kristen, and you weren't so much friends with the younger gals. You had more of a mentor-mentee relationship." And to a certain degree, a case can be made for that; these relationships included a lot of mentoring. When I met with the Emmanuel Lutheran ladies outside of Bible study, I'm quite certain I shared more of my struggles and worries and fears with them than they shared with me. In my memory, our relationship didn't reflect reciprocity. Yet they mentored me within the confines of this Wednesday morning group at church and at get-togethers, not through school or a job. Our time wasn't goal-oriented.[1] It was relaxed with a give-and-take feel to it, even if the give-and-take wasn't always fifty-fifty.

When I sobbed through my fears that sending my sons to public school could be spiritually detrimental to them (it wasn't), they didn't shame me or roll their eyes over my dramatics. They listened and told me that if God placed it on my heart and my husband's heart to send them to public school, then He would see to it that they were fine. And they backed that up with advice on how to keep Christ at the center of our family culture regardless of where the boys went to school.

To me, this was the very definition of friendship. Through them, God spoke to me and cared for me in powerful ways.

Perhaps it's futile to debate semantics. At the end of the day, I think the beauty of bookend friends is that they are both mentors *and* friends. What makes a good bookend friend is what makes a good any type of friend: sharing some sort of common interest, even if that common interest is as simple as the well-being of each other and each other's families.

Dr. Timothy Keller talked about how friendship requires a foundation of common love that's discovered rather than created. That foundation must be built upon, but the foundation itself is something both folks realize is there; they don't create it from scratch. It must first "be discovered before it can be forged."[2]

He went on to weave a quote by Ralph Waldo Emerson into his own words, saying, "Friendship does not ask, *Do you love me?* so much as *Do you see the same truth? Are you passionate about the same thing?*"[3]

A friendship develops out of something deeper than two humans taking up the same space. The friendship itself has to be *about* something—a common interest. Small children may simply ask, "Will you be my friend?" of another, but even young'uns need something to be the oxygen that keeps supplying the life of the friendship. That may be mutual affection for baseball, Barbies, or baby animals. That shared interest will be what grows the friendship. Otherwise, young or old, "there would be nothing for the friendship to be about."[4] It may be about singleness, marriage, homeschooling, your public school's PTA, a mutual pain over prodigal children, or your mutual desire to grow in your faith. But it has to be something.

And this mutual love isn't dependent on both friends being the same age or in the same stage of life.

Scripture models the value of this kind of mother-daughter or older-sister relationship through the Titus 2 woman who lived by example and didn't distract from the gospel (vv. 3–6). In the book of Ruth, we see how Ruth, the daughter-in-law of Naomi, blessed and supported Naomi through her words and actions. Consequently, Ruth was put in the path of a distant family member, Boaz, whom she married. And by doing this, she was placed in the direct lineage of Jesus, becoming His great-grandmother. Ruth and Naomi's intergenerational friendship positively impacted the history of every believer in Christ.

Bookend friendships continue to positively impact my future. Fifteen years after that Bible study, when my twin sons left for college, the ground shifted for me, causing everything that felt normal before to feel off. Friends who had been there before me, like Connie and Kathy, assured me that all my topsy-turvy feelings were quite common. They reminded me that a new normal would settle into place.

And they were right.

And so goes the biggest blessing of bookend friends: They listen to you and assure you that where you are right now is normal, and the way you feel right now won't be the way you feel forever. Bookend friends are true "iron [that] sharpens iron" friends (Proverbs 27:17).

Here's to standing tall together, walking toward a more hopeful future.

HOW TO BE A GOOD FRIEND TO OTHERS

When looking for friends, consider women who are
a life stage or four ahead of you or behind you who'll
enrich your present-day life through wisdom and energy.

CHAPTER 14

WHEN A FRIENDSHIP ENDS WITHOUT YOUR SAY-SO

Instead of waiting on an apology, wait on the Lord, [and] be of good courage.
GRACE VALENTINE

I bounced into the nail salon one April, excited to give my nails a little springtime lovin'. A new-to-me nail tech with curly, dark hair framing beautiful brown eyes met me and delivered a warm greeting. She waved me back to her station, and I happily took a seat in the white leather chair. After a bit of small talk, she asked me if I was getting my nails done for a special occasion. I told her that I wanted a nail spruce-up before taking a trip with a friend. "Oh," she responded, matter-of-factly, "I recently took a trip with a friend, but . . ." Her brown eyes bobbed up to mine and back down again. "It didn't go so well."

I furrowed my brows and responded, "Oh, I'm so sorry to hear that. If you don't mind me asking, what happened?"

And that's when she poured out her story, ripe and fresh as if it'd happened that same week.

Her friend—let's call her Emily—was my nail tech's best friend and roommate. She and her parents invited my nail tech—let's call her Bella—on a cruise to the Caribbean. Bella was thrilled to be invited and planned her heart out for all sorts of Caribbean adventures. Emily seemed excited to share this experience with her bestie, too, and both girls reveled in all the fun activities the cruise offered.

All was well until day three of the cruise when, suddenly, Emily became distant and aloof. Bella repeatedly asked what was wrong and if she had done something to offend her. Emily insisted she hadn't, yet her behavior wouldn't warm toward Bella. By day five of the trip, Emily coldly told Bella that their friendship was over. Bella, stunned and devastated, spent the remainder of the cruise on outings by herself or crying alone in her cabin. As soon as she returned home, she moved out of the apartment she had shared with Emily.

At the point in time when Bella shared this with me, she still had no idea what had caused Emily to suddenly and inexplicably do a 180-degree turn on their friendship. Emily's behavior went beyond ghosting. It veered into cruel territory that was without conscience.

To a certain degree, I could relate to Bella's story. When I was a freshman in college, during my very first semester, I became friends with a fellow music major, a senior named Patricia. We got along swimmingly, regularly sharing everything from our meals to our thoughts on Mozart to our interest in various good-lookin' males spotted across campus. After finals of my first semester, we exchanged Christmas gifts along with sentiments like "I'll miss you over break!" and "See you in January!"

Once Christmas break ended and I returned to campus for the second semester of my freshman year, I called Patricia while unpacking my suitcase because I was excited to see her again. When she didn't answer, I assumed she wasn't back on campus yet or was doing some new-semester grocery shopping. I certainly didn't worry that anything was wrong.

However, when I saw Patricia on campus the next day and offered her a greeting that she barely acknowledged, I began to think there might be a problem. After extending a couple of invites her way that she flatly refused, my suspicion turned to confirmation that, indeed, there was a problem.

Over the next several days, I asked her six ways from Sunday to please, please, *please* share with me what I had done wrong and why she was mad at me. I asked her every question I could think of in hopes of getting to the bottom of whatever issue she had with me. I felt desperate to make things right again.

My questions met only silence. No communication of any kind came my way, let alone answers to my questions.

I won't exaggerate the severity of the ordeal by saying this was as devastating a loss for me as Bella's loss of Emily's friendship was for her. I certainly valued my friendship with Patricia, but she wasn't my best friend or even the only friend I had on campus. I'd only known her for about three months, not for decades. At the same time, this was a *very* bitter pill for me to swallow. I have a tender heart the size of Texas, and sometimes I think God placed my telltale ticker on the outside of my exoskeleton. As an Enneagram Two whose currency is relationships, I *hate* to be on the outs in any of the important familial or friend relationships in my life. To not know why I was on the outs with Patricia felt like torture.

Between taking nineteen credit hours that semester and immersing myself in other parts of campus life, I stayed busy and distracted. At the same time, Patricia was an important friend to me, and in the weeks following our friendship breakup, I frequently lamented the loss of our relationship. At night as I tried to sleep, old fears resurfaced and slithered around me. At best, I'd surely done something to cause Patricia's change of heart. At worst, I was unfriendable. I figured I'd better doubly watch how I treated my other friends lest I lose them too.

As that semester drew to a close, I decided to give Patricia a peace offering of sorts, so I sent her a graduation gift. Alongside the thank-you note for that gift, Patricia positively stunned me with not only an apology for her treatment of me that semester, but also an explanation for her change in behavior toward me. I don't remember what the letter said exactly, but I do remember her mentioning that as a senior, she felt embarrassed to be hanging out with a freshman. So she'd thought it best to cut ties with me.

I responded that I forgave her, and I wished her well in all her future postgraduate endeavors. I meant it too. I harbored no anger or malice toward her for a couple of reasons. First, thankfully, I continued to make friends in college that semester, and I began dating David, so time and other relationships helped me see that I wasn't relationship repellant. Second, I simply felt awash in relief that her problem with me wasn't really about me after all. It was about her own insecurity of gal-palling with someone four years her junior.

While this is true, I know today that it's possible there were other reasons Patricia didn't want to hang out with me. Generally speaking, the difference in maturity between eighteen and twenty-two is huge, and I know I was a young eighteen. Maybe I had personality traits that were more quirks than perks, and that may've played into her desire to ditch me. I have no idea.

Either way, did that justify her dropping our friendship like it was too hot to hold? To go from being fully engaged in our friendship to fully estranged seemingly overnight? Nope. But she apologized for it, and a well-placed apology truly can cover a multitude of sins. I put the matter to rest then and there and haven't thought about it much since then.

Of course, that's easier to do when you do hold an apology as well as answers in your hands. As far as I know, Bella hasn't been afforded the benefit of either one. She holds only questions and more questions.

And that can be the hardest part of a friendship breakup: All the inevitable questions may never receive answers.

If Bella's story mirrors a slice of your own friendship story, first let me say how sorry I am. You deserved better, and no personality quirk warrants being left out in the relational cold with no explanation. Your friendship loss is particularly acute and devastating, and it leaves a gargantuan hole in your heart. And yet, know that whatever caused your own friendship breakup, it likely wasn't about you.

As you process this, may I gently offer a suggestion for how to proceed from here? Pivot your questions from those that have no answers to those that do.

When a friendship ends without your say-so, what does God—the Creator of your singularly beautiful heart and soul—say is true about you?

"Nothing in all of creation can separate you from the love of God" (Romans 8:35–39). God loves you and will never leave you.

When your friendship circumstances change for the worst, what do you know won't change?

"Jesus Christ is the same yesterday and today and forever" (Hebrews 13:8). He is dependable 100 percent of the time.

When questions and fears about the future of your friendships keep you up at night, what can you rest in knowing is true?

God says, "Never will I fail you or abandon you" (Hebrews 13:5). He will never leave you, period.

Will you be able to forge friendships that last?

"If God is for us, who can be against us? He who did not spare his own Son, but gave him up for us all—how will he not also, along with him, graciously give us all things?" (Romans 8:31–32). God didn't spare His own Son for us, so He'll spare no cost to bring us what (and who) we need. Jesus coming to us, dying on the cross for us, and being resurrected to life with us brings this truth full circle in our lives.

Reciting and rehearsing truths about our Father in heaven and our Friend Jesus will fill our friendship holes and make us whole—in spite of a whole lot of unanswered questions.

Of course, sometimes a friendship unravels slowly and over time. It happens without your permission, but it's a slower change than the sudden-death nature of being cruelly dropped, ghosted, or canceled.

Following the global pandemic, I didn't have work friendships to the same degree I had before. While I still enjoyed great relationships with friends in the work lane of my life, many of the relationships I'd worked hard to cultivate in the previous decade weren't what they had been. Several people I'd grown up with in the internet world as awkward, gangly writer-teens now traveled in different directions from me.

Natural changes that come with age, stages of life, relational gains and strains, and perhaps shifting belief systems were partly in play. Like leaves on a tree, friendships either change and grow or change and fade. This reality is a natural part of life, and it means that quite often, there's no good guy or bad guy. We're simply going to grow closer with folks or more distant.

Drew Hunter writes, "Many friendships also change over time. . . . We don't require every friendship to last a lifetime. If friendships weren't fluid, we would each stay locked into the three closest friends we made on the fourth-grade playground."[1]

These work relationships were yet another example of changing friendships. The only thing I could do at this time was remind myself of the truth that God always gives His best to me, and even if I didn't know why some of those friendships had changed and faded, it was a part of a good plan, not a bad one.

In her book *Mostly What God Does*, Savannah Guthrie gives beautiful language to this perspective:

> I've always felt believing in God isn't really the hard part; believing he is good and actively engaged in our lives and the world in the face of so much pain—that is the hard part. God does not require us to ignore or gloss over the sorrows we experience or the injustice we see but to believe past them. Believe that he is on the case, that his intentions toward us are good, that he is ever inclined toward forgiveness and reconciliation. That the pains of this world are not his plan and will not be how the story ends.[2]

As is the case with so much loss and devastation in our lives, we must walk through our friendship losses by taking proactive steps *to believe past* them. So when a friendship ends without our say-so, we believe past it. Our current pain and sadness are a chapter of the story, but not the end of it. And that story will end on a redemptive note.

What's more, I wouldn't be where I am today without those friendships then, and I can be thankful for that.

A turnaround in your friendship discouragement could be right around the corner—either in circumstances or in your perspective of your circumstances. The Holy Spirit sees you and hears you where you are in your diminutive and drastic friendship losses today and has great things in mind for your future.

God's reserves of mercy and comfort stretch higher and deeper and further than any season of discouragement. While it's good and right to deeply grieve your friendship loss that left you heartbroken and lonely, ask the Holy Spirit to fill you with a sense of expectancy about your future friendships. God's heart is for you to have friends. Never underestimate how far He'll go to faithfully fulfill that promise.

While I don't know every detail of your friendship breakup, I do know we're broken people ourselves living alongside broken people in a broken world. And all too often, what shouldn't happen—what we don't want to happen—is exactly what does. Yet God specializes in bringing dead things to life. You never know when He could do some divine heart surgery for your friend, and she comes to you with an apology of her own. Maybe not. But it's my prayer that one day you'll be able to think back to that time and be thankful that in some small way, what happened then, difficult as it was, has miraculously brought you to where you are today, with the people you're with.

After facing a dramatic series of personal losses including a betrayal, author Phylicia Masonheimer wrote the following words based on the old hymn "Farther Along": "Farther along, I'll know all about it. For now—I only know that God is still good."[3]

The friendship may've ended without your say-so, and you may never know why. Farther along, you will. But today, you can be content in knowing that it did have God's say-so—it was no surprise to Him. Farther along, the Lord will restore what the locusts have eaten (Joel 2:25). You will come out the other side of this too.

HOW TO BE A GOOD FRIEND TO OTHERS

When a friendship ends without your say-so, pivot from your questions with no answers to those with answers and believe past the losses and pain to know that God will bring redemption from your friendship breakup. You may not have answers today, but farther along, you will.

CHAPTER 15

REJECTION SUCKS, BUT DON'T LET IT SUCK YOU DOWN

We worship the status quo. Yet
growth comes in endings.
MARY DEMUTH, *THE SEVEN DEADLY FRIENDSHIPS*

When my kids were young and we moved frequently as a military family, each child had their own way of dealing with the news about our next move. Generally speaking, all three of them were sad about leaving where we were because after three-ish years in one place, they'd made friends and felt like they belonged. But the way my kiddos expressed their sadness and regret differed.

In varying degrees, two of my kids would verbally communicate their unhappiness. They'd say things like these:

"I'm so sad we have to leave."

"Why does Daddy's job keep making us have to move?"

"I really wish we could stay. I like my friends here and don't want to make new ones."

My other child, however, would do no such verbalizing—at least not in his younger years. Instead, he would simmer, stew, and generally act like a turkey to his family members. Without uttering a word about the move, he'd let us know exactly how he felt about it. As one who hadn't signed up for a job that required frequent moves, that child would take his frustration and pain out on those, like his parents, who in one way or another had signed up for the job.

While my husband and I didn't enjoy our child taking his frustration and pain out on us, we understood why he did. After all, David and I had a part in creating the environment where frequent moves were part of the picture. But when it comes to folks who've endured the painful reality of rejection, some make other people pay the price for the pain they experienced, even though they had no part in creating it.

Indeed, rejection is a part of life that every single one of us must learn to maneuver in healthy ways.

No matter how long you've known someone, something definitive might happen to break up your friendship, such as a betrayal or broken trust. Or as the people within a friendship change, so does the friendship itself. There are so many circumstances that can cause a friendship to end.

And yet, the kind of friendship breakup I described in chapter 14 between Bella and Emily is happening more frequently these days: the kind where one friend ends it seemingly overnight. At least, I'm coming across stories of it more often. By and large,

I'm not talking about friendships that have just gotten off the ground. I'm talking about those that have been running strong for years, if not decades. One moment, these friends sit firmly in the ride-or-die, sister category. In the next, one friend cuts off all communication with the other, often without explanation.

Why is this happening? Is it due to some kind of pervasive "the grass is greener" belief about friendships that makes folks cut and run? Is it due to immaturity or an avoidance to settling conflict? Are more people, out of their own fear of rejection, rejecting others first so they won't be rejected themselves? I don't rightly know, and perhaps only God knows. But *great day*, the way it happens, especially when done without a reason, frustrates me to no end.

If this has been your reality at any point in your life, I'm so sorry. As Anjuli Paschall noted after a few friendship breakups, "Each [rejection] has sliced off a part of my soul."[1] Rejection can feel like someone has plunged a knife into your heart and twisted it. It'll make you mad at yourself for not seeing it coming. Even though you did nothing wrong, or nothing beyond the more commonplace errors or mistakes, it can still leave you drowning in shame. This is especially true if you've been rejected by one who spoke vows in front of God and everyone to never reject you "till death do us part." And yet, when friends you considered family reject you, the pain is terribly acute as well.

Just as friendships are in some cases ending in dramatic, unexplainable fashion, some folks are handling the *rejection* that comes from friendship loss in dramatic, unexplainable fashion. That is, *they're not handling it well.* And while this is certainly not a way to be a good friend to yourself, it's also a way to set yourself up to be a terrible friend to others.

It's bad enough to experience the pain of rejection. Rejection sucks. Of course it does! But don't let that pain push you to a place where you crap all over other people—especially those, including your other friends and loved ones, who had no part in what happened to you in the first place. Don't let rejection suck you down to a place where you behave contrary to who you know you are as a person of integrity and character.

Listen, I'm all for coping with your sadness in the short term by gorging on a pint of ice cream, bingeing *Ted Lasso* in one weekend, or buying two new pairs of shoes. I'm certainly not above soothing myself through a vice or two.

In the long term, however, instead of dealing with the real loss and genuine sadness and anger from rejection in healthy ways, folks will react toward others in unhealthy ways. For example, if someone is missing the friendship of a former friend, she may come on rather strongly with a potential new friend she meets. And when the other person pulls away from the intensity, the rejected one hurts all the more because the other person isn't filling the space her former friend left. She internalizes it as just another rejection, and from that pain she gets mad and proceeds to malign the other woman.

Doing this allows rejection to steal, kill, and destroy a double portion beyond what it did in the first place. In the words of author Melanie Shankle, "Your new friend can't pay for the sins of your old friend."[2]

Your new friend isn't responsible for your old friend's careless behavior. We must stop looking at other people, including our friends, to fix our friendship devastation from the outside in and remember that only Jesus can heal us of painful rejection from the inside out. Jesus will work through our friends to comfort us and speak truth, absolutely. But placing our trust in Him gives us a satisfying dose of peace and perspective—like that of knowing the rejection may've been more about them than us.

Of course, rejection would be easier to take if it was a

one-time experience. Instead, rejection is a repeat offender in all our lives. As a reader of mine wrote to me, "Kristen, to be honest . . . I cannot take one more rejection."[3]

When rejection after rejection arrives on our doorsteps, it doesn't take long to get to the end of our ropes and our patience. Gun-shy about others in general, we're tempted to slam the door on life with people, period.

But here is where we find the fork in the road: We can either take steps to process the rejection in a healthy way so we heal, like through journaling or with a trusted friend or loved one, or begin to see ourselves as a victim of it. If we go the victim route, we allow the pain experienced to bubble over till we react out of our pain toward the women who rejected us. Or we do so toward others in our lives.

While we may experience greater or lesser consequences from rejection depending on the circumstances, that doesn't give us license to behave like donkeys. Is rejection demoralizing? Embarrassing? Painful as all get-out? Yep, yep, yep. But it's not the end of life; it's a part of it for each and every one of us.

So instead of becoming emotionally stuck in the pain of rejection, we need help getting unstuck. Nicole Zasowski, a real-deal marriage and family therapist, says there are three reasons we may be emotionally stuck in our pain:

1. "We are waiting for the person whose words and actions created the wound to correct their harmful message. Sometimes this does happen . . . but we have no control over this and if we wait for this moment to pursue healing, we might be waiting a long time."
2. "We are waiting for someone else to enter our lives (a significant other or a friend) to correct what someone else broke from our past. Relationships are profoundly

147

helpful to our healing. But love from the outside alone is not powerful enough to heal our pain on the inside."

3. "It's never occurred to us that we have been given agency to participate in our healing . . . and claim a truth, act on that truth, and wait for the feelings to follow."[4]

Considering Nicole's advice, what can we do to put rejection at the hands of friends in a proper, healthy place? How can we mourn the trouble it brought into our lives without letting it create more? We set ourselves up for success by treating rejection as a part of life—something every single person has to deal with—and not as the end of life as we know it.

DEALING WITH REJECTION AS THE END OF LIFE SAYS: I will slander the one who rejected me and malign her every chance I get. I won't physically harm her, but I'll murder her reputation six ways from Sunday.

DEALING WITH REJECTION AS A PART OF LIFE SAYS: I may speak about the friendship breakdown and my feelings about it with a trusted loved one, friend, or therapist, but I will not trash the one who hurt me, privately or publicly.

DEALING WITH REJECTION AS THE END OF LIFE SAYS: I will act as if she's dead to me. However I perceive she hurt me, I'll doubly hurt her back.

DEALING WITH REJECTION AS A PART OF LIFE SAYS: I don't like what happened, but I will pray God's best for her as I pray His best for me. I will put my efforts toward strengthening myself, not sabotaging her.

DEALING WITH REJECTION AS THE END OF LIFE SAYS: I will carry this hurt and loss into my other friendships either consciously or unconsciously and therefore make them and other loved ones pay for the sins of the former friend who rejected me.

DEALING WITH REJECTION AS A PART OF LIFE SAYS: The only

person I'll hold accountable for my rejection is the person who rejected me, and I'll keep praying that I not only learn from this experience, but that God will help me forgive her (Luke 23:34).

DEALING WITH REJECTION AS THE END OF LIFE SAYS: I will encourage a victim mentality by ruminating on how I deal with rejection more than anyone else does.

DEALING WITH REJECTION AS A PART OF LIFE SAYS: Because rejection is a part of life, I can let it turn me into a victim of my circumstances or a victor over them.

DEALING WITH REJECTION AS THE END OF LIFE SAYS: I'm done with friends. When "friends" treat you this way, who needs enemies?

DEALING WITH REJECTION AS A PART OF LIFE SAYS: I'll continue to build and strengthen my friendships because the only way to guarantee never having friends again is to never try making friends again.

Treating rejection as a part of life and not the end of life as we know it keeps our hearts in a place of kindness and humility rather than bitterness and pain. Then we can act from those healthy places. So if we cross paths in the Target parking lot with the one who rejected us, we can offer her a smile and a simple greeting. If her name comes up in conversation with someone else, we can choose not to bad-mouth her. We can even lift her up behind her back as we would want her to do for us.

This isn't dependent on whether or not others behave kindly toward us.

On the popular show *Ted Lasso*, Ted is an American football coach who's hired to coach the English soccer team AFC Richmond. As coach, he also mentors a fellow named Nathan Shelley. Under Ted's leadership and direction, Nathan transitions from being the equipment supervisor to a fellow coach. Sadly, he also transitions from being a friend of Ted's to a self-appointed adversary. He publicly maligns Ted every chance he gets. And yet, Ted treats "Nate the Great" with respect and dignity no matter how Nate behaves in return.

We can make like Ted and do likewise.

More importantly, we can make like Jesus, who went through periods of His life when His friends disappointed Him (Matthew 26:40). He knew the sting of rejection by Peter, a close friend in His inner circle, right before He died on the cross (Luke 22:54–62). And yet, after Jesus rose again, He appeared to the disciples, including Peter, as they fished one morning. Jesus called out to them, "Friends, haven't you any fish?" (John 21:5).

The disciples answered no, but after following Jesus' instructions about where to cast their nets, they rowed ashore with a literal boatload of fish. Jesus, who had prepared a fire, cooked some of the fish and fed the disciples breakfast.

The convicting part of this story is that even though Peter had rejected Jesus, Jesus still called him "friend."[5] Did Peter want to be brought back into the fold? Yes, he did. He regretted rejecting Jesus. Your friend may never regret rejecting you, but we can still model Jesus' choices and be friendly in return, regardless of their actions. As Proverbs 18:24 says, "A man who has friends must himself be friendly" (NKJV).

I want to carry about me a friendly demeanor, not a bitter, resentful one. That doesn't mean we don't place boundaries where needed, of course. It just means we're not going to let the one who rejected us take more ground from us.

Not only is rejection a part of life, but I believe that in God's redemptive hands, it can also be a *gift* of life. I say that with all the tenderness that my heart can hold, and as one who's faced repeated rejection by a loved one who shouldn't have rejected me once, let alone over and over again. And just the same, I know this to be true: Rejection is a redirection that is ultimately a part of God's plans for us.

Consider these wise words from Lucretia Berry: "Therefore, I don't have to take rejection personally. I simply get to rest in hope that rejection invites me to a clearer, more focused direction toward that which has been designed and orchestrated specifically for me."[6]

Rejection also invites us to a more focused direction toward the ones God has orchestrated specifically for you and me as friends. A definitive no in one direction reveals information we didn't have before. It is our invitation to turn our attention elsewhere.

Also, it's worth mentioning that we should be evaluating our circumstances to see if every relational heartbreak we've labeled as a rejection has been aptly named. Brené Brown says it this way: "Don't walk through the world looking for evidence you don't belong, because you'll always find it."[7]

While rejection is a difficult thing we all face, we don't want to go looking for it. Sometimes folks haven't rejected us; they're just not inviting us into their lives. There is a difference between the two. No matter how we've met with a friend's ambivalence or rejection, we can grieve our real losses, pray for perseverance and healing, talk with a trusted person about our feelings, and get back to work investing in our other friendships.

Rejection sucks, no two ways about it. But let's not allow it to turn us bitter or cynical. We can still be friendly in our words and actions—using boundaries as necessary—so rejection doesn't suck us down. We can trust God to deal with the other person and ask Him to help us deal with what is ours to deal with. We can bravely stay softhearted so others are drawn to us still.

And we can trust Him, knowing that no matter how rejection

enters our lives, we can persevere through it and be stronger because of it.

HOW TO BE A GOOD FRIEND TO OTHERS

Rejection sucks, but when you see it as a part of life and not the end of it, you won't let it suck you down.

CHAPTER 16

YOUR TOP-NOTCH TOOL FOR BUILDING YOUR FRIENDSHIPS

Ritual and ceremony are powerful
bonding tools. They result in a sense
of community, a feeling of unity far
beyond what you might expect.
DEL SUGGS

M y darlin' daughter is a competitive tennis player, and her favorite pro has long been a Spanish phenom named Rafael Nadal, or Rafa for short. She'll faithfully get up at all hours of the night to watch him play tennis from tournament locations across the world. Often looped in with Roger Federer and Novak Djokovic as the Big Three, Rafa is one of the best players the world has ever seen. Personally, I don't just love watching

153

him for his wicked forehand shots. I love his integrity, kindness, and the discipline he demonstrates on and off the court.

Part of his discipline is displayed through his many, *many* customary rituals that occur before, during, and after a match. From the way he walks onto the court to the way he arranges his water and energy drinks to the way he tugs on his shirt before each serve, the fella does love himself some routines.

In his autobiography, *Rafa*, Nadal explains the why behind his rituals: "[They are] a way of placing myself in a match, ordering my surroundings to match the order I seek in my head."[1]

Rafa has won a staggering twenty-two Grand Slam titles. While some may say his rituals are rather obsessive, it's hard to argue with results. They haven't hurt his end goal of being one of the best tennis players in history.

Now, most of us are not quite so . . . *diligent* when it comes to specific rituals we keep for the daily, weekly, or even yearly events of our lives. I don't have the goal (or the talent!) to be an outstanding tennis player, but I do want to build outstanding friendships. And there's something to be said for allowing rituals to positively influence that end goal.

Rituals Help You Consistently Spend Time with Friends

I've discovered that when it comes to our friendships, rituals can be the fuel that feeds them. Rituals will help us regularly get together with folks, which will in turn help us regularly grow our friendships.

For three years and some change, I had the privilege of being a member of the "Juniper bunch," a group of seven friends who met simply because we were all neighbors on or around the same street: Juniper Court. During those years we lived together in Albuquerque, New Mexico, we were the reliable, all-hands-on-deck people for our wee-watts and for each other. After collectively moving from Juniper Court to various parts of the country, these fellow military-spouse friends and I developed a tradition of a yearly trip together to keep up with one another and to encourage each other in marriage and parenting. Just because we all scattered hither and yon didn't mean we wanted to stop investing in our friendship.

Plus, these trips, which we often took during long seasons as solo parents, gave us a well-deserved break from the constant demands of raising little people.

So every year for over a decade, we convened for a trip. Sometimes every single one of us could make it, and other times life caused one or more of us to miss out. But we didn't let that stop us from trying to make it the following year.

Usually, we took our trips during the bleak month of February, treating ourselves to a bright-spot-on-our-calendar getaway under that month's gray skies. Keeping our trip at the same time each year meant our spouses had plenty of time to take off from work or figure out childcare. Quite often, one of us would act as host of the trip. That is, we'd all travel to a place where one of us was stationed, and the person who lived there would make the lodging arrangements and chauffeur us around. Because February is considered off-season for many places in the continental United States, we'd usually get a killer deal at some kind of bed-and-breakfast, hotel, or retreat center.

Our destinations, such as Solomons, Maryland; Hot Springs, Arkansas; and Grand Lake, Oklahoma, weren't what you might call sexy—except that year some of the gals visited me in Hawaii. But they were comfy, cheap, and cheerful. And really, who cares about the environs when all you want to do is gab and eat and go on walks and gab and eat some more? Especially when you get to do it without little people interrupting you to take them to the bathroom *again* or tattle on their sibling *again* or to bring out more snacks *again*!

Those times together were sweet because we got a much-needed break from the daily grind. But they were also sweet because they served as touchpoints of connection that kept our hearts tied to one another. The benefits stretched beyond those long weekends as they strengthened our hearts for the rigorous demands of military life waiting for us back home.

Because of the realities that have come with changing life seasons, we don't regularly take those trips anymore. Who knows, maybe we will again in the future! Whether that happens or not, I'm thankful for all the good ways those trips served me and my family at that time.

That's an example of a friendship ritual enjoyed *yearly*. I also have rituals I employ to encourage my friendships *monthly*. While in-person time will always outshine digital time, I'm not about to give up the advantages of digital connections with friends who live outside my town of Colorado Springs. So I have monthly phone dates to catch up with Alli. And I have monthly Zoom calls to discuss life and work projects with Holley. When I'm on a call with these gals, it's my goal to schedule the following month's call before we hang up. That way, it's on the calendar and we don't have to think about it again. In the past, I've had video calls scheduled with friends at, for example, 11:00 a.m. on the second Tuesday of each month. However you decide to regularly meet up for conversation, it will feel easier to keep those dates because half the work involved in getting together is a done deal.

Last, I also use rituals to build my friendships on a *weekly* basis. Again, because spending time together in person is the best way to feed our friendships, rituals do the most good when we're interacting with our local people. And the more consistently we can get together with a local friend or two, the more those friendship will grow.

For the past eight years, my friend Aimée and I have had weekly coffee dates. Well, it's coffee for her and tea for me because I don't like coffee. But I digress! Anyway, these dates began as a way to reconnect after originally meeting fifteen years earlier (see chapter 4). On a Sunday morning, Aimée asked if I'd like to meet sometime that week for coffee, and we made plans right then and there to meet the following Friday afternoon. On that coffee/tea date, we got along like a house afire, chatting about everything from friendship to facial moisturizers. And from that moment on, we made those coffee dates a weekly event, often keeping them on Fridays (as our schedules allow) because that gives us something to look forward to after the long workweek.

Sometimes we meet at one of our houses instead of out and about. During COVID and even today, if one of us is under the weather, we meet in empty parking lots, sidling up to each other in our cars and talking through the driver's side windows.

Whenever and wherever we meet, we share and talk about ev-er-y-thing. We allow each other to see further inside than most, and our talks are a type of therapy for both of us. As my yearly trips with the Juniper bunch served me in the past, my time with Aimée serves me in the present by making me a better wife to my husband, a better mama to my adult kids, and a better all-around human.

Another weekly ritual of mine is attending yoga and Pilates classes with my friend Rebecca. Not only do we keep our perimenopausal selves healthier by stretching and strengthening our bodies, but we get to regularly talk and connect after the class.

While none of my friendship rituals have been lifelong, they have all been life-giving in their seasons as they helped me grow my community. And such is the gift of rituals. Rituals strengthen relationships because proximity and consistency nourish a friendship's longevity. Just as a friendship could end because you're no longer in proximity with one another, doing something to encourage proximity can strengthen that friendship. Whether weekly, monthly, or yearly, rituals help us connect with friends more readily because their regular placement on the calendar helps guarantee they'll happen.

Rituals Are Time-Magic for Friendships

Erica Bauermeister writes, "A ritual is a form of time-magic. It takes the endless flow of life and slows it down long enough for us to pay attention, to put the stamp of our experience on an otherwise ephemeral moment."[2] As discussed in the early part of this chapter, rituals and friendship go hand in hand to create that form of "time-magic" where each person can have their soul and heart fed through connection and encouragement on a regular basis. In keeping with this, I have a personal ritual that I like to think creates additional time-magic for my friends: creative gift giving.

As you've undoubtedly learned by this point in the book, I've not always made choices that have served my friendships well. But one thing I *have* done well is pay attention to what my friends say they like and don't like. Then, if there's an inexpensive, doable way to extend a thoughtful gesture in keeping with something they like, I extend it. For example, a friend of mine mentioned in a conversation that she liked cherry pie. So when we had her family over for dinner, I made cherry pie for dessert (I've bought it before too). Another friend loves sweet tea, so in the summer I try to have a small pitcher of it in the house when she visits.

Will Guidara writes, "Gifts are a way to tell people you saw, heard, and recognized them—that you cared enough to listen, and to do something with what you heard. A gift transforms an interaction, taking it from transactional to relational . . . and the right one can help you to extend your hospitality all the way into someone's life."[3] For me, actively paying attention to my friends' interests and then doing something for them related to that interest is my ritual of extending hospitality one small, relational gesture at a time.

A very easy way to consistently keep this ritual is for your friends' birthdays. After hearing my friend Rachel say she loved hydrangeas, I stumbled upon a cute notepad and pen with hydrangeas on them, and I gave them to her as a birthday gift. My friend Aimée doesn't love camping, but her husband does. So I know she loves to bring what creature comforts she can on those camping trips. One year, an acquaintance I follow online, Sophie Hudson, brought to my attention an outdoor chair that comfortably rocks back and forth. Since it was a big birthday for Aimée, I bought it for her, and she loved it.

Now, this is where you may be thinking, *Uh, Kristen? It's common sense to buy people what they like for their birthdays. Obviously, I'm not going to buy them what they don't like.* Fair point! But we all know how easy it is to get that generic candle or gift card for someone instead. And while there's no shame in either (in fact, I've often given both as gifts and I *love* to receive them!), there's something special about giving folks something personal and a bit off the beaten path that really lets them know they're important to you.

Also, my budget is such that I can't give a birthday gift to every friend I have. But what I *can* do is take a few moments to write them a card or text or to sing them "Happy Birthday" via a voice message and tell them how glad I am that they were born. I'm a words-of-affirmation girl whose very favorite gift is a card with friendly sentiments inside. I'll take that over diamonds any day. And while a lot of folks aren't words-of-affirmation people, I've discovered that everyone still loves receiving written words of kindness that make them feel seen and valued. Those gifts offer priceless affection for zero dollars.

Of course, thoughtful gestures "just because" are great too. When the son of one of my friends was in a car accident and she had to pick him up several hours from home, I wanted to help but wasn't sure what I could do. Then an idea came to me. While I've been an empty nester for a couple of years now, I still can't break the habit of cooking more food than my husband and I need. That night, I'd made two ham and cheese quiches for dinner, so I decided to take the second quiche to her house. My friend has a large family, and I knew that the quiche wouldn't go nearly far enough to feed all of them. But I thought it might help a little, so I dropped it off just the same. Later that night, my friend texted to say it was just what she and her son needed when they arrived home famished.

My friend Maria often makes huge batches of homemade granola. I am wild for her granola and could swan-dive into a bowl of it! So she often brings me extra in empty pickle or canning jars. Again, she's giving from her extra at minimal or no cost to herself but to great benefit for me.

Sometimes a little forethought about how we can give from our overflow goes a long way to bless and build our friendships. The ritual of giving an unexpected, simple gift, no matter how small, is like waving a magic wand that, to reiterate Will Guidara's earlier quote, "[extends] your hospitality all the way into someone's life." I'll add, too, that it extends hospitality to someone's heart as well.

Here are some practical points to keep in mind so rituals serve you and your desire to strengthen your friendships:

- Rituals help us connect with friends more readily because they do the thinking for us. For example, if you and your friend decide to regularly meet for lunch or dinner on the third Thursday of the month, the work of scheduling a date is done for you. You know not to schedule something else during lunchtime. Tweaks and changes will naturally happen as life happens, but scheduling a meetup or a ritual and committing to it is half the battle!

- Let the fun factor be the rationale behind your ritual. Aimée and I like to gab and drink coffee and tea, so our regularly scheduled get-togethers happen in a relaxed setting that encourages conversation. In your own ritual-making, do what's fun for you and your friend.

- Discuss with your friend(s) your baseline requirements of your get-togethers *and* the purpose for them. Doing this increases the odds for consistently keeping your scheduled friend dates. Consider your schedule limitations when setting dates and locations.

- Keep expectations in check. This ain't the mafia; rituals serve you and your relationships, not the other way around. And they do that by becoming guardrails that work with limitations to help you grow your relationships. In the words of Eugene Petersen in *The Message* translation, Jesus said in Scripture He "prefer[s] a flexible heart to an inflexible ritual" (Matthew 12:7). If one or more persons can't make your meetup because of family commitments or complications, give them grace. If coffee or dinner dates can't be kept because someone is out of town, no big deal! Keep expectations relaxed so you don't suffocate all the joy out of your rituals—and therefore your friendships.

Research shows that rituals "can help to reduce anxiety

symptoms and stress associated with uncertainty. Having rituals to look forward to can be grounding and reassuring in turbulent times, by providing us with a sense of predictability and consistency. . . . Rituals also have been shown to improve social cohesion and connection, helping to improve trust among ritual group members."[4]

Rituals are a top-notch tool for building your friendships. They provide regular touchpoints for fostering trust and connection between yourself and your friends. They give you a consistent platform for you to share vulnerably and listen compassionately.

Drew Hunter writes, "It's true that friendships often begin without effort. But that's not how friendships endure."[5] All friendships take work, but why not be a good friend to yourself *and* your gal pals by making the work easier for everyone all the way around?

HOW TO BE A GOOD FRIEND TO OTHERS

When you commit to regular calendar dates for getting together with friends—be that once a week, a month, or a year—you discover that rituals are a top-notch tool for building your friendships. They help you strengthen your friendships by doing the thinking for you.

CHAPTER 17

I LOVE MY FRIEND TO PIECES, BUT I DON'T LOVE HER VIEWS ON _____

*Love is not the same as agreement
or approval, but love dictates HOW
we go about disagreement.*
PHYLICIA MASONHEIMER
AND PRICELIS PERREAUX-DOMINGUEZ

As a teen, I had a character flaw that stuck in my parents' craw more than anything: my love of arguing. If one of them felt the need to discipline me for something, I'd promptly turn into a lawyer for my own defense and passionately attempt to justify what I'd said or done. I'd argue and argue with a personal goal of getting the last word. I was slow to learn how this propensity never won my parents over to my point of view. They wouldn't be manipulated or swayed. And once they handed out a punishment, there was nothing for me to do but serve the time for my crime.

On one such occasion, after my poor daddy undoubtedly felt like he'd gone ten rounds in a boxing match with a mouthy teenager, he sighed loudly and said, "Kristen, do me a favor and never become an actual lawyer, because you'll always be held in contempt of court for arguing with the judge."

Even though I hated the punishment, which usually meant losing phone privileges, I did enjoy arguing. (Perhaps you could file this story under "Tell me you're a strong-willed firstborn without telling me you're a strong-willed firstborn.")

In my twenties, I sometimes chose to pick a fight with someone—even a friend—over opposing viewpoints. That is, I might needle someone till she decided to rumble with me. Eventually, both of us having our say would lead to an argument. Then we'd eventually apologize, and everything would be fine till the next rumble.

This was the cycle with a couple of friends in my life till one day when it dawned on me how dreadfully unfun it was. So I decided then and there to stop engaging in that behavior. Of course, it helped that shortly after that I had a very impactful conversation with a good friend of mine, Barb, who was one of those wise bookend friends from Emmanuel Lutheran in Ohio.

After lamenting to her about a conversation I'd had with a friend where differing opinions took over, she told me something I've not forgotten: "Kristen, you can be right or be in relationship, but you can't have it both ways."

Well, if you're a gal like me whose currency is in relationships, that'll make you straighten up and take stock of your behavior right quick. I dearly want my important relationships to stay in good shape. To that end, the only behavior I can control is my own.

For a long time I've not had the interest or energy for arguing that I used to have. Now, I don't shy away from conflict with my closest loved ones if I believe it's necessary to work through something. But generally speaking, conflict makes me nauseous. And arguing with friends over politics, theology, or a host of other topics is of no interest to me. I don't mind discussing tricky issues with people in person, as long as it's civil. But the day you catch me doing that on the internet is the day I've been held hostage and forced to do it. (So please send help!)

Does that mean I don't care about certain issues anymore? Hardly. I care deeply about a lot of topics. But I'm not going to let my opinions about those topics drive a wedge between my heart and the heart of another. I'll no longer sacrifice or damage a friendship for full (and sometimes flawed) argumentative communication. I care more about our connection than being correct.

By excavating further down in my own heart, I've also come to see how my tendency to argue had another deeper problem at play: pride. Hannah, the mother of the prophet Samuel in the Old Testament, said these convicting words about pride:

> Do not keep talking so proudly
> or let your mouth speak such arrogance,
> for the LORD is a God who knows,
> and by him deeds are weighed. (1 Samuel 2:3)

The Lord will always get to the basement-level "why" of our actions, and for me, letting my love of aired opinions outweigh my love of people all came down to pride. Would I rather deal with the humbling reality of not fully expressing my opinion or deal with the Lord humbling me in some way because I wouldn't humble myself?

In their *Decision 2024* guide, coauthors Phylicia Masonheimer and Pricelis Perreaux-Dominguez write, "The heart of a prideful person is closed off to the perspectives of others. Remember: listening does not equal endorsement, but it does pave the way to understanding."[1]

When we posture ourselves to listen, we're automatically paying attention to the other person, which in turn paves the way to understanding them. In doing this myself, I've come to see why some folks think differently from me. That doesn't mean that after I've listened to them, I suddenly agree with them. But it does mean I've heard them out and, more often than not, better understand where they're coming from—even if I still don't see eye to eye with where they're going.

Also, when we listen to others, we elevate them instead of ourselves. And this is how we love people well and engage with people respectfully and with dignity, regardless of what we think about what they're saying. Jesus described Himself as "gentle and humble in heart" (Matthew 11:29). That's the opposite of prideful, and it's a good way to conduct ourselves around others.

It's well and good to go into an encounter with a listening posture. The problem is, however, when that conversation escalates in intensity. Someone's feathers get ruffled, and suddenly the room's atmospheric pressure changes faster than a politician changes their mind. Perhaps the conversation remains civil; perhaps it plummets along with everyone's good mood.

What do we do then? Well, I can tell you I often respond with something my sister taught me: "You may be right about that." Or I may say something like, "You bring up a good point." Or, "You've given me something to think about." I'll keep my comments truthful and respectful but mild so they douse water rather than dump gasoline on any smoldering embers.

I think about the best way to keep first things first: I try to understand where the other person's coming from, not mowing her down with what I think or believe through a defensive emotional reaction.

I've been on the other end of someone who talked constantly about her beliefs, and those conversations usually aren't fun because they're completely one-sided. Without the discipline of listening going both ways, it becomes mighty draining (and uncomfortable) for the one doing all the listening. Also, when someone spends the majority of her time stating her opinions on every possible headline out there, it can come across like that person just likes to hear the sound of her own voice.

Often, I think we take issue with the way someone chooses to communicate something more than we do with the actual viewpoint they communicate.

In his book *The Four Loves*, C. S. Lewis quoted Ralph Waldo Emerson in asking, "Do you care about the same truth?"[2] Lewis went on to write, "The man who agrees with us that some question, little regarded by others, is of great importance, can be our Friend. He need not agree with us about the answer."[3]

We don't have to agree with our friends or think the same way as them to love them well. I think I used to believe it was my unofficial job to make someone—like my poor daddy in my teen years—come around to my point of view by crafting just the right argument so they would be convinced. I acted like I had something to prove, which is mighty wearying to the listener. Now I don't waste my time on that. I've come to believe what Pastor Dominic Done wrote: "If you're just looking for someone who thinks, acts, looks, speaks, and votes like you, it's not another person you're describing, it's *yourself*. But friendship isn't found in mirrors; it's found in the celebration of difference."[4]

Amen. If I'm only willing to be around someone who thinks, acts, looks, speaks, and votes just like me, then one of us would become unnecessary. I doubt that a like-minded identical twin exists for anyone.

Treating those we disagree with respectfully and with dignity seems mighty countercultural these days. Our division is deeper and wider than the Grand Canyon, and not just on hot-button issues like abortion, theology, and vaccine policy. Contentious division exists on stuff the general populace shouldn't care one whit about, like whether a particular mother-of-the-bride's dress outshined her daughter's wedding dress.[5] We've got big feelings and big opinions that we're too inclined to share in big ways, even if what we're weighing in on is none of our business.

What *is* our business is considering what mountain is worth dying on: clashing with the other person or connecting with them.

> What *is* our business is considering what mountain is worth dying on: clashing with the other person or connecting with them.

Now when I find myself having a conversation with someone whose ideology feels like it's coming from another world, I picture Jesus standing there with us, reminding me that "Your love for one another will prove to the world that you are my disciples" (John 13:35 NLT).

And I remember to let my words and actions come from a kind and loving place. That doesn't mean I never challenge another person's statement. If I believe the Holy Spirit is urging me to kindly and gently offer an opposing viewpoint, I'll do so judiciously. But I think of it as a drop shot in tennis that's lightly placed just over the net, not as a forceful serve that's fired across the net from back at the baseline. When I keep this imagery in mind, usually the conversation proceeds with civility and grace. But on the rare occasion it doesn't, I'll choose to set my racket down altogether by ending the conversation with, "I appreciate where you're coming from, and I thank you for sharing your viewpoint with me." And I let that be that.

Oswald Chambers wrote, "Never try to make your experience a principle for others, but allow God to be as creative and original with others as He is with you."[6]

When facts about a friend grate on our nerves, it helps to remember that God works just as creatively through her as He does through us. The thing that annoys us about our friend today could be the thing that He uses to draw us closer to her tomorrow. As I've experienced in my own life, there's something about bonding through differences—rather than only in spite of them—that can make a friendship almost impenetrable. Sturdy and strong are the roots of a tree that's weathered many a storm.

Sturdy is the friendship that endures through theological and political storms, and other storms as well.

Today, I often still need help in knowing what to say or do—or not say or do—regarding differences. But young Kristen learned, and old(er) Kristen continues to learn, that the idea of setting someone straight, no matter how wrong I think they are in their beliefs, is a faulty move that often leads to faulty actions because it's not rooted in love. It's rooted in (say it with me now!) pride.

Not only do I not let differences divide my friendships; I don't let differences keep me from making new friendships. I don't let them keep me from reading books by people whose viewpoints on any number of things may differ from my own. I'm not really interested in hanging out exclusively in echo chambers. Plus, rubbing shoulders with others of differing opinions, whether or not those differences come up in conversation, helps me practice what I preach about being "right." Because it's easy to practice conversational humility and hold my tongue when I'm with people who generally think like me. But the rubber meets the road when I'm around people who don't.

Yes, there's a season for everything—a season to speak up and a season to sit on it. But at the end of the day, I want to err on the side of grace by loving my friend with gentleness, humility, kindness, and respect. I want to remember that we don't write people off because of our differences. Jesus picked disciples and friends who didn't make sense on paper; they were a ragtag group that represented opposing political viewpoints. And if He sat in the middle of those folks, it's good for us to do it too.

I don't have to love everything about my friend. Odds are good she doesn't love everything about me! But I'll love her *through* our differences. I won't cancel her or our friendship because of them. I'll care for and nurture that relationship rather than sabotage it by having "my big important say" on fill-in-the-blank.

I will love her well by being quick to listen, slow to speak, and certainly slow to become angry (James 1:19). And I'll remind myself, *An unexpressed opinion—no matter how rooted in facts I believe it to be—is still a valid one.* Really, it's a small price to pay for keeping relationship over being right.

And that feels right too.

HOW TO BE A GOOD FRIEND TO OTHERS

You don't have to agree with your friend on A, B, and C to love them well. May your love for them move you to interact with them respectfully and with dignity. And may you care more about your connection with your friend than being correct.

CHAPTER 18

LEAVE ROOM FOR MISTAKES

*Expecting perfection makes it easy to write
people off. While relationships certainly
need standards of kindness, respect, and
consistency, they also need grace and
forgiveness. Because any relationship that
lasts long enough will have highs and lows.*
KARI KAMPAKIS

Alli and I became fast friends when we both lived in Hawaii.
She's the most loyal of the loyal friends who'll go to bat for
you no matter what Goliath stands between you and her. She's
also as thoughtful as they come and will do things like send you
a surprise gift because she saw it and thought you'd like it. She'll
pray the mountains off their chain on your behalf. She's also honest to a fault, but in the kindest of ways. One day, she came up to
me after church and said, "Now Kristen, you always look darling,
but I'd be happy to give you some makeup tips, if you'd like."

Because she delivered her sentence in the most disarming way, I couldn't be offended. I knew Alli loved to play with cosmetics, so I immediately responded, "Why yes, I would!" I didn't know what I was doing with any of it, and I really didn't mind a little help.

One Saturday afternoon, I went over to her house with my makeup, per her instructions. She met me with her sunny smile, warm as our island home. After leading me to her dining room, she asked me to set my makeup on the table. I laid my foundation, eye shadow, blush, and mascara out in front of her. And then my eyes widened as she sat her makeup on the table. While mine fit in a small pouch, hers filled up an expandable tackle box that a pro bass fisherman would've coveted.

I still laugh out loud when I think about that.

Alli kindly showed me how to do all the makeupy things, including filling in my eyebrows and applying eyeliner, and today I still reap the rewards of her lesson back then.

Because Jesus loves me this I know, the Lord kindly arranged it so Alli and her family moved to Colorado Springs a few months before my family did. So when we relocated to a home not ten minutes from hers, both families enjoyed picking right back up in our high-altitude town where we'd left off on our sea-level island.

As my kids grew and entered middle school and high school, I found myself in that life territory where my home address might as well have been the Honda minivan. During that time, I lived in the car, driving kids not only to their respective schools but also to swim lessons, drum lessons, precision air-rifle team practice, theater practice, tennis practice, youth group, student council meetings, and JROTC practice.

As a result of life punching the gas on my home and work schedules, it slammed the brakes on my social life—or rather any energy I had to regularly foster a social life. This meant I didn't reach out to friends as often as I had before. Not because I didn't want to hang out with them, but between managing the kids' schedules, my home, my job, and some difficult circumstances with the health of extended family members, I didn't have the energy to think up where to go and what to do with whom.

Alli, who was a parenting season ahead of me, recognized the stage of life I was in and totally took the reins on our friendship. For about three years, if I got together with Alli or if our families got together, it was because she did the asking every single time. In that season when I often felt like I was underwater, breathing through a straw, I couldn't accept her every invitation to get together. But I could sometimes, and those times were life-giving.

In that season of overwhelm, she was a safe harbor for me, and our friendship grew as she humbly and faithfully reached out to me on the regular.

Alli could've made a different choice. She could've been annoyed or upset that I wasn't reciprocating her invites with invites of my own. She could've placed demands and expectations on me. She could've passive-aggressively commented that I wasn't giving enough to our friendship. As the expression goes, "We have time for what's important to us." While that's true, it's also true that seasons can drain you so you're unable to do all kinds of things you'd like to do. Because Alli did most of the inviting, she also did the work of planning the details. Therefore, getting together felt more doable and less overwhelming to add to my plate.

Alli was grace personified to me. She didn't criticize the fact that, right or wrong, our friendship was rather lopsided in that season. She simply made herself available, gave me a safe place to be me, and loved me well regardless of how little I reciprocated.

I wasn't the most generous of friends during those years, but she overlooked my limitations and didn't give up befriending me.

Eventually, when the curtain closed on that crazy-busy time in my life, I was able to respond in kind once again.

This brings up an interesting topic: At what point is it okay for one friend to do the work of two in a season, and when is it not okay?

I'm a hardworking girl who doesn't give up easily. This has served me well in the past, like when I was parenting a strong-willed kiddo bent on pushing a boundary again . . . and again. But my dog-with-a-bone mentality hasn't always benefited me well in friendships.

For example, at the beginning of a potential friendship I'd really like to see work out, I'll reach out to the other person and invite her to do this or that. That's well and good when the other person is interested in forming a friendship with me. But if she's not, it becomes apparent through her lack of reciprocation. Instead of seeing that for what it is, I've been known to double down by reaching out to her more often. In short, I'll begin doing the work for the both of us. Now, as was the case with Alli and me, it's possible that the other person isn't reaching out because she's busy. Perhaps she doesn't think to do so or is very shy. It may take time for the Holy Spirit to lead you in deciding if this is the place you should invest your time.

But more often than not, I've found that when this happens, I need to read the writing on the wall and accept that this friendship probably isn't meant to be. When I do that, I can stop investing energy in that person when my energy would be better spent on another friend.

This begs the question, How can I wisely spend my energy so I receive maximum benefits from what I do put into my friendships?

Answering that question is as nuanced as the topic of friendship itself. In a long-held friendship, I may spend more time reaching out to another friend if I know this friend is going through a particularly difficult time. When someone's life is in triage, it's simply being a good friend to check in on her more often than you might otherwise. In your own conversations and time together, it's good to let her have the floor more often to share what she's going through. Seasoned friendships call for periods when the scales of give-and-take are off-balance.

Generally speaking, I've learned that whether a friendship is just getting off the ground or has been a part of my life since high school, it shouldn't *always* be lopsided.

And if it is lopsided because the other person shows little to no interest in a friendship with me, I'm going to honor her choice to go in a different direction—the same choice we all want to have. Also, I've found freedom in saying to myself, *Kristen, she's just not able to reciprocate right now. Maybe she won't be ever. Either way, you're gonna be fine.* By doing this, I take the pressure off myself (and her!) and just let us both be. And then I trust our good God to bring me the friends who will enthusiastically return my hand of friendship by welcoming my efforts and responding in kind with their own.

Now, that isn't to say I don't still make bona fide friendship mistakes that do not serve my time and energies well. For example, I'm chronically late to places. I'm one who's always trying to wring every last second out of a minute in any given hour of the day, so I often pack too much into my schedule. Inevitably, this causes me to run late.

Certain members of my family and friend group believe that if you're on time, you're late. I do not ascribe to that mantra. So you can imagine how much these friends and family members enjoy this aspect of my personality! I've inconvenienced and maddened them because of my careless regard for the clock—and their own busy lives.

A clear example of how this caused me to be a bad friend was when my daughter was in middle school. Late for an after-school meeting, I speed-walked through the crowded front of the school, making my way toward the entry. An acquaintance of mine was walking slowly toward me, so I said with more per-functory politeness than perceptiveness, "Hey! How are you?"

She responded, "I'm not good."

I stopped long enough to give her a sympathetic look and said, "Oh, I'm so sorry to hear that."

There was an awkward pause where I waited for her to go on, but she didn't. Since I was late, I told her something generic like, "I hope things get better soon. I'm so sorry I have to go . . . I'm late for a meeting." She gave a weak smile, then turned the other way to leave.

Now, this woman and I were friendly to each other, but we weren't friends. Still, if I hadn't been running late, I could've used our encounter as an opportunity to connect further, because while she was slow to speak, I felt that she wanted to. Perhaps that point of connection could've turned into a real friendship. I'll never know because we never crossed paths again.

I could tell you other stories about friendship mistakes too, like when I've not given friends the benefit of the doubt—a sure-fire way to strangle the life out of a friendship if ever there was one. I can tell you about when I've been unreasonably contrary. I've been selfish, shortsighted, and just plain cranky. Many friends would've kicked me to the curb over my friendship mis-steps, and really, some probably have. But thankfully, many of my friends are the kind who leave room for bad moods and mistakes.

Sadly, I think our culture today doesn't have much patience for normal human mistakes. While toxicity or someone chron-ically mishandling our hearts requires firm consequences and boundaries, we need to leave room for the natural ups and downs of relationships. We don't want to turn the occasional slight, forgotten text, ignored invitation, or season of lopsided friendship into a mountain when it's really a molehill. We need to extend grace in our friendships and not give up on them or throw them away over everyday, garden-variety mistakes and limitations.

Unless we immediately see enough red flags to fill a Texas amusement park, we don't throw in the towel at the first sign of a problem.

Pope Francis observed that we live in a "throwaway culture" laced with disposable relationships.[1] We give up on folks when they fall short of perfection. The problem is, we're all sinners who fall short (Romans 3:23). And I can't help but wonder if a lot of our loneliness these days is because we've given up on friendships—or viewed the natural highs and lows that any relationship goes through as being the end of the road rather than a simple speed bump along the way. We'd serve ourselves and others well by looking at our friendships with more wisdom and discernment. Not doing so means we risk discarding something that is largely meant to bless us.

If a string of mistakes is starting to grate on you, it's time to be a grown-up and have a conversation about it rather than stew on it or systematically cancel or ghost the other person. I've had a friend or two graciously do this to me about my tardiness problem, and it made me change my behavior as I stared in the face of how that behavior negatively affected them. Scripture reflects this by telling us to take our problems straight to the offender (Matthew 18:15).

When someone's mistakes bother us still, author and speaker Jennifer Rothschild talks about literally saying the word *grace* out loud in response to our feelings. "When you're offended, 'grace.' When you're ticked off, 'grace.' . . . When you're disappointed, 'grace.'"[2] That word, *grace*, can act like a deep breath that continually recenters us so we don't react because of a bad day or a bad mood and elevate something of no real consequence into a real problem.

Alli and I have been friends for more than fifteen years now. We've had plenty of opportunities to cover the other's mistakes and shortcomings with grace. And because of it, we enjoy the satisfaction that can only come from longtime, loyal friendships.

As I referenced earlier, on the show *Ted Lasso,* Kansas-born Ted coaches an English soccer team. A natural leader, Ted is exceedingly friendly and refuses to give up on befriending his boss, Rebecca. When a coworker mentions Rebecca's intimidating personality, Ted says, "She's got some fences, all right, but you just gotta hop over 'em."[3] For Ted, his persistence pays off as he and Rebecca do become good friends. He doesn't let her early frostiness affect his efforts toward her. The time, energy, and kindness he puts into that endeavor are worth the work.

Sometimes, we must evaluate for ourselves, with prayer and guidance from the Holy Spirit, whether our time and efforts are worth putting into a particular friendship. Sometimes they are, sometimes they aren't. But let's not be trigger-happy and shoot down a possible friendship over something impossibly little in the grand scheme of things.

On our own, we're not strong enough to turn around a culture that's so unforgiving of mistakes. But in our own circles, we can spend our time on friendships that yield fruit for us and them. We can show up and make the decision to offer grace more readily—because heaven knows we need it too.

HOW TO BE A GOOD FRIEND TO OTHERS

Don't throw away quality friendships because of everyday human mistakes. Spend time with those friends who value you and reciprocate your friendship overtures.

CHAPTER 19

MAKING FRIENDS BY SHOWING UP

Vulnerability is not winning or losing; it's
having the courage to show up and be seen
when we have no control over the outcome.
BRENÉ BROWN, *RISING STRONG*

After we moved to Albuquerque, New Mexico, a neighbor invited me to an established monthly Bunco group—typically a group of twelve members who play a dice game together. The members of the group take turns hosting the game night, so everyone has an opportunity to open their home to others. Not being familiar with Bunco or the biggest fan of games in general, I thought about declining. After all, I'd already banked a gazillion game-time hours playing Candy Land and HiHo! Cherry-O with my tiny twin sons. But I said yes to joining the group because I thought maybe it would help me jump-start making friends in our new city.

It turns out I genuinely *loved* those Bunco nights. I loved the people, the conversation, the way we laughed in a raucous way that bubbled past our front doors into the neighborhood. I loved the food each person brought and the way we usually had enough leftovers to turn into lunch for ourselves and our kids the next day. I even loved the game of Bunco itself.

I didn't become great friends with every girl in the group, but those game night get-togethers provided a way for me to be around others consistently. And that led to me forming a few friendships, some that are still a part of my life today.

Several years later, when my children were in elementary school, I chose to support their teachers by volunteering in the kids' classrooms rather than joining the PTO or PTA. Since I'm allergic to energy-depleting meetings and enjoy the opportunity to get acquainted with my kids' teachers, this worked well for me. (Of course, I'm mighty thankful for those folks who *do* participate in and lead parent-teacher school organizations!) Ultimately, I formed a beloved friendship with another mom, Jamie, who regularly volunteered in the same classroom. In choosing an activity that didn't zap me, I met a friend who energized me, because being near her felt like being plugged into a light socket. And since we both didn't mind showing up in that way to help, we both kept showing up and enjoying each other's company. Eventually, we began getting together outside the kids' classrooms too.

My yes to both Bunco and classroom momming weren't hell yeses. I was perfectly fine with doing them, but I wasn't gung ho about them on the front end. But time would prove that sometimes you can offer a lukewarm yes that turns into a fired-up yes. These are two examples of when that was true for me. Because when we want to make friends, the goal of showing up isn't to feel 100 percent excited about what you're going to do. It's to make the commitment to show up and see what you find. It's the commitment to first give something a try and then wait for your feelings about it to catch up. And if they never catch up, it's the commitment to show up again somewhere else.

In my first book, *Girl Meets Change*, I briefly mentioned how showing up, opening up, and praying up are helpful ways to make friends in times of change. In this chapter and the next two, I will go into a lot more detail about how these principles really are the fastest roads to finding friends, whether you're in a season of rowdy change or calm familiarity. They are the highways to friendship, even if while traveling their long, continuous routes, you wonder if you've accidentally taken a wrong turn down a dead-end road instead.

Right about now you may be thinking, *Well, Kristen, I'm so glad these situations worked for you. But I've showed up at a lot of places, and it hasn't worked out for me. Not only that, but I've consistently "showed up" places only to leave feeling rather beat up by women.*

If that's you, first and foremost I'm so sorry this happened to you once, let alone repeatedly. I would also say that I can empathize with you. Remember how I said in the first chapter that in trying to make friends, I've swung the bat and missed a lot? Well, I also know what it's like to feel like someone grabbed the bat out of my hands and used it on me—or at least on my heart. My circumstances around their disappointing or mean behavior may differ from yours, or they may be the same. Either way, this singular truth remains: The work of making friends *is* going to bang up and bruise you from time to time.

And this is true whether we're talking about literally showing up at physical places to meet friends or metaphorically showing up for our friends to grow our friendships. To avoid this is to avoid friendships (and relationships in general). Sometimes, we give what we have to a relationship in an effort to love others well, and yet, in the end, we get burned. Author Holley Gerth writes about this as she encourages us not to let our own doubts or the fickleness and poor decisions of others convince us to give up on people.

> What if you miss something else? The reality is you probably will. But if you spend your life scanning the horizon for danger, how will you ever move forward? . . . Pain is sometimes the unfortunate price we pay for living fully, loving deeply, daring to dream. Yes, you can choose to make it your mission to protect yourself from now on. But your life will become smaller, narrower. It will have less room for unpredictable things like love and hope. . . . You're wiser now. . . . You have learned, grown, become stronger than you were before. Use that. Be fierce and tenderhearted at the same time.[1]

You and I can't afford to let the ugliness of humans convince us that making friends isn't worth the time and effort. Accept that in the same way that raising babies is hard and buying a car is scary and furnishing a house or apartment is expensive, making friends is hard in that it will require you to keep showing up again and again. It doesn't matter who you see on so-and-so's social media account that makes it look so easy for her. Most likely, 99.9 percent of the time it's been hard for her too. Accepting this will encourage you to keep putting yourself in proximity to others to increase the likelihood of finding people you connect with as friends. If you do this, success will eventually come if you don't quit too soon.

I bet actor John Krasinski, otherwise known as Jim from *The Office*, would agree with me on this. John originally aspired to be an English teacher. Then he attended the National Theater

Institute, a rigorous training program in Connecticut for hopeful actors.[2] He was there because he had some college credits that had transferred, and the program showed him that acting was what he really wanted to do.[3] With this career shift in mind, John made an agreement with his mom that if he didn't feel his new profession was headed anywhere in three years' time, he would pull out of that career plan.

Two and a half years later, John was living in New York City and hating the daily waiting-tables grind that is the life of an aspiring actor. So he called his mom. After relaying how terrible things were going for him, John asked if she could come get him.[4] His mom replied, "You know, it's September, wait till the end of the year. Don't give up just yet."[5]

He stayed, and three weeks later he landed the role of "Jim" on *The Office*.[6]

John had to continually fight insecurity, fear, and discouragement to keep showing up for auditions. He received who knows how many rejections in his early journey toward acting. He didn't just show up and—*boom!*—get hired. He persevered and didn't give up, even when he wanted to. Even when he thought the writing was on the wall that he should.

Perseverance pays off in a lot of life circumstances, and it certainly does in making friends.

So, dear one, don't stop showing up to places where potential friends could be. Filling your own role at that event, organization, or gathering may introduce you to someone who becomes one bang-up friend.

While showing up where women are is so often required to get a friendship off the ground, research shows it takes spending fifty hours with someone to be a casual friend, ninety hours to be a real friend, and two hundred to three hundred hours to be a close friend.[7]

Showing up repeatedly is a productive practice for building those hours.

Now, you may be able to shave off a few of those hours toward building a close friendship with someone if you immediately hit it off in a profound way (like I did with Maria). But generally speaking, there are no shortcuts to circumventing the work that building a close friendship requires—or the hours it takes to get there.

That part of friendship isn't complicated, but it isn't easy, either, because of the intentional time and effort it requires.

So how do you show up in the way you know you need to but don't always want to?

You keep in mind the following equation:

AN ACTIVITY YOU ENJOY

+

SHOWING UP TO THAT ACTIVITY REPEATEDLY

=

OPPORTUNITY FOR MAKING FRIENDS

When you consider showing up at activities you enjoy, you create win-win opportunities for connection. For example, I love good conversation that has the potential to delve below the shallow waters of small talk. (That's a building block for a close friend, by the way, and why it takes two to three hundred hours to become close friends with someone.) Because I love getting to know folks, I like to do something that provides a platform for conversation.

I also love cheering for my friends' kids. When my daughter became a committed tennis player, I became a committed tennis fan myself. When my friend Maria's son, Krue, began playing tennis, I asked them both if they'd mind if I watched some of his matches. They didn't mind, and I had the win-win of showing up to watch a sport I truly enjoy while also spending time with a friend I truly enjoy. And I had the opportunity to cheer for Krue, who's an amazing fella himself. So what I had there was a win-win-win!

The objective of showing up isn't to slam your calendar with places to visit or groups to join. It's to pick a few great options that gel well with your schedule and interests. Here are some ideas for where to show up and meet potential friends:

- Attending church and sitting in different places
- Inviting someone to eat at a restaurant or at your home after church or work
- Visiting church groups, communities, or Bible studies
- Showing up at regular times at the park with your kids
- Participating in local groups for moms
- Attending story time at a bookstore or library
- Volunteering for a nonprofit, at your kids' school, for their sports team, or for their homeschool group (For years, my father-in-law volunteered as a "grandpa" reading buddy at his neighborhood elementary school. He loved it!)
- Asking someone you met at the gym to be your exercise buddy
- Joining a local book club or adult sports team
- Joining a class that covers your area of interest, like a language, painting, or dance class

Readers and friends of mine have relayed to me their success at finding their own friends in these additional locales:

- At Airbnbs or hotels where they were staying
- At water parks

- At the dog park
- In the bleachers at sporting events
- Within writing or community-theater groups

Here are some ways to show up for a gal who is already your friend with the goal of deepening your relationship:

- Initiating get-togethers at favorite locations you both enjoy, like a coffee shop, restaurant, or your favorite hiking trail
- Bringing her a meal after she's had a baby, moved to a new house, undergone surgery, experienced illness, or suffered the loss of a loved one
- Bringing her chocolate chip cookies or brownies just because you know she likes that particular treat
- Texting her a "Just thinking of you" note
- Sending her a card in the mail
- Attending the sporting events or special events of her kids. (My friends Rebecca, Connie, and others have done this often, and it always makes my heart swell!)
- Attending a weekly exercise class with her
- Vacationing together on a girls' trip or together with your families
- Cheering for her and crying with her

Of course, our places of employment are great settings to make friends too! But to move those friendships from casual to close, it'll help to show up at places outside the work environment. While you're still likely to talk shop at dinner or on that walk together, you're also more likely to introduce other topics of conversation into the friendship.

When deciphering where to show up in an effort to find

friends, and more importantly, with whom, consider these wise words from Lauren, a reader of mine: "I have found a lot of freedom in allowing myself to strictly pursue relationships that are energizing to me. . . . Regardless of how desperate for friendship or lonely I may feel, if I don't click with someone or trust them, I do not need to put pressure on myself to continually make efforts to connect with those individuals."[8]

When it comes to finding friends, we want to find those who give us energy rather than take away from our already limited storehouses. So if you're showing up somewhere that isn't working either people-wise or activity-wise, by all means show up at an alternative with alternative people. In turn, this will encourage you to give more than you take as well.

Yes, sometimes we're called to be in community with difficult, energy-depleting people. It would be selfish and naive to live like that's not true. *But* we shouldn't be spending most or all of our time and energy on those folks. While making friends is genuine work, as is so much in life, it should ultimately be a task that rewards you with people who energize you.

Listen, I know as well as anyone that as I put in the work to show up to places and with people I want to grow friendships with, the effort can still feel mighty taxing. It'd be great if God would simply make it happen for us!

Around the time when Jesus was calling His first disciples, He was preaching at the lake of Gennesaret when He noticed two boats at the water's edge. Getting into the boat belonging to Simon, Jesus asked him to row a bit out from the shore. On the heels of that request came a second one: "Put out into deep water, and let down the nets for a catch" (Luke 5:4).

Simon answered, "Master, we've worked hard all night and haven't caught anything. But because you say so, I will let down the nets" (v. 5).

As Simon Peter lowered the nets into the sea, I wonder if he rolled his eyes to the sky. At that point of the morning, he was haggard from fishing all night. If it'd been up to him, he'd have packed up and gone home, rendering this fishing excursion a bust. Even though it didn't make sense to him to keep trying, Peter did try again because Jesus told him to try again.

Because You say so, I will let down the nets.

And that brought big results.

I love what author and teacher Priscilla Shirer says about this passage.

Jesus . . . could've said, "Fish! Get in the boat," and the fish would've just started hopping into the boat from everywhere. Instead, He said, "Peter, cast out your net. I got fish for you, but in order for you to get them, you've got to participate with me in the process." . . . What is God asking you to do? . . . How is He asking you to show up in the scenario? Whatever He's asked you to do, do it . . . and trust Him that if you throw out this net, there's going to be reward the likes of which you cannot even fathom.[9]

When Jesus enters any equation, what seems to be wasted time turns into time well spent. It's vulnerable to keep showing up places with people, but that's how we place ourselves in position for big results.

Jesus wants you to have your friends, but He wants you to participate in the process. Trust Him by showing up vulnerably.

HOW TO BE A GOOD FRIEND TO OTHERS

God will bring you to your friends, but you must do the work of participating in the process by showing up where potential friends may be.

CHAPTER 20

MAKING FRIENDS BY OPENING UP

Shame dies when stories are told in safe spaces.
ANN VOSKAMP

While I now love hosting people at my house, I wasn't always that way. If I did venture to extend an invitation, I also believed I needed a sparkling house to adequately host other people—if not a few new furniture pieces to boot. I had to learn that imperfection *is* perfection when it comes to having people over, because ain't nobody feeling like they can relax and have a good time in a stainless, sterile house-museum.

In addition to showing up where people are—and showing up *for* your friends—opening your home and your heart are wonderful ways to boost your friendships.

But I didn't always know this, especially the opening-up-your-home part.

When we lived on base in Albuquerque, David and I invited

our friend group, who happened to also be our neighbors, over for dinner. As the date of the dinner approached, I panicked, largely because I believed our house wasn't in top-notch form for this gathering. But I still wanted to get together with the folks we'd invited over. So what did I do? I called Rebecca, my friend who lived across the street, and asked if she could host. I told her I'd bring all the food if only she'd do all the hosting. So not only did I invite myself and my family over, but I also invited a dozen other people over to *someone else's house.*

Lest this be news to anyone, that is not the best move in how to be a good friend. Instead, it's a pro move in how to take advantage of your friends. Thinking back, I find it doubly ridiculous because each and every one of those families in our friend group who were coming over lived in the same kind of house that I did. We all lived in cookie-cutter base duplexes that were as run-of-the-mill and unsexy as they come. They had Formica countertops in the kitchen and linoleum floors throughout the *entire* house—not a lick of carpet anywhere (unless you brought some in yourself). They had backyards that, left to their own devices, grew sand burrs instead of grass. We all had the very same imperfect houses, not to mention young kids skilled at lowering the bar on a put-together home. If there was ever an optimum environment for cutting your teeth on having people over, that was it.

But because Rebecca is gracious, she said yes, and we still laugh about how she threw my party that evening.

Listen, there's nothing wrong with divvying up entertaining duties by asking others to bring food to a get-together. There's nothing wrong with one person doing most of the cooking while another handles most of the hosting or other locational prep work. If that's mutually agreed upon early on, then fabulous! But it *is* a problem if you throw your own responsibilities onto your friend at the eleventh hour so she has to scramble to do what she didn't sign up to do in the first place.

If I had a personal insignia or emblem, it would say, "Making easy things difficult since 1974." And in my younger years, I had a ridiculous propensity to overcomplicate having people over. Why? Because I struggled with being vulnerable—and you know what feels vulnerable? Opening up your house to people not related to you.

There's something very personal and exposed about letting people within the four walls of our homes. I think this is because opening up our homes is often the first step in opening up our hearts.

If you show up somewhere—say, at a painting class or a restaurant—to meet someone, you're showing up with simply yourself. But if you invite someone into your home, they're seeing much more of you—your likes, your interests, your style (or lack thereof, you might think), and your temperament. There's a lot more there for someone to examine, and you may worry you'll be judged as coming up short. Or at least I did. Now I know that if someone *is* judging your home, she's missing the whole point of an invitation in the first place. But I think most of us don't really care about what another person's house looks like. We're simply thankful for the invitation to enjoy another's hospitality.

Still, there's no getting away from the fact that our homes tell others a lot about us. And in my midtwenties as a young wife and mama, the cost versus benefit of putting a lot of work into my house while not being able to control what someone thought of it (or me) felt like high cost, low benefit.

And I mitigated the cost by imposing on Rebecca. It was the only time I did that, though, because it felt worse to put that on her than it did to risk being judged negatively.

So how did I get to the place where I was comfortable having people over? Well, I think that came about in two different ways.

First, I learned to define my purpose for inviting people over.

In her book *The Art of Gathering*, author Priya Parker challenges us to look at the purpose of our gatherings; that is, to ask what the desired result of our get-together is.[1] It may seem as if this could complicate a simple gathering like a dinner among friends. I mean, we're hosting a barbeque or pizza dinner, not a board meeting. But if I'd asked myself what the purpose of my gathering was back in Albuquerque, I could've saved myself from acting on insecurities that genuinely did complicate the get-together. Answering that question would've simplified the mission of our meeting.

So I defined my purpose for having people over as such: To get to know our "family away from family," not to show off my house.

Second, I saw other people live out their own defined purposes, whether or not they sat down to officially define them. I witnessed Rebecca and other friends in that neighborhood, like Mary, Cheryl, Amy, and Jen, host with a warm, easy-breezy attitude. Watching them model this made the whole thing much less intimidating to me. These friends showed me that the main purpose behind opening up my home was to provide a platform for connection, not commendation. It was about building relationships, not my own ego. Therefore, opening up my home to others felt less vulnerable because it wasn't about me, how well my kids behaved, or the state of my home. It was about creating a comfy, welcoming environment for the guests and my family at the same time.

When I simply thought about how I could make everyone in my home comfortable, I realized having people over is quite easy.

So now, when I have people over, I keep in mind three

principles I learned from author Myquillyn Smith: boundaries, priorities, and people.[2]

Boundaries

In the past, I've paid a hefty price for not considering boundaries more carefully.

Our sons were (and still are) LEGO lovers. When we lived in Hawaii, we kept all their completed LEGO projects on a high shelf. Since we often had families with young children over, this was our way of keeping those beloved belongings out of reach and in one piece. Other bins of LEGOs lay within easy access for kids to enjoy.

One evening, we hosted a party celebrating a big promotion for David, and we invited over several friends and their families. At some point during the evening, one of the other dads took James and Ethan's cherished LEGO Star Wars Slave 1 ship off the shelf and gave it to his young son.

That child proceeded to disassemble it faster than you can say, "I have a bad feeling about this."

My sons don't mention many grudges from their younger years, but believe me when I say that they've never forgotten the systematic dismantling of the LEGO ship (and a few other favorite projects), as well as the dad who allowed it. While that dad should've known better, I wish in retrospect I would've put those LEGO sets clean out of sight so they would've been out of mind too. But you can bet your Imperial Star Destroyer that for future evenings involving company with kids, I hid the completed LEGO sets. Boundaries for the win!

Today, I still keep boundaries in mind by closing the door of my husband's office so young'uns stay out. And I might shut our bedroom door if I've put something in there, like a stash of birthday gifts or a collection of household items for a kid's apartment, that I don't want anyone to mess with.

Also, boundaries show up by what I'm meals willing to make, usually a selection from a rotating list of tried-and-true recipes that are easy to prepare and delicious to eat.

The overall point, I think, is that it's more than okay to have boundaries in your own home. Just because you're having people over to enjoy one part of your house doesn't mean those folks need to have access to everything. Because your home isn't a museum, you don't have to offer a tour . . . unless you want to! And they'll be thrilled to enjoy whatever meal you serve because it's a meal they didn't have to cook for themselves!

Priorities

I keep my priorities straight for having company over by prioritizing my purpose for the dinner first. Sometimes, I envision it front and center, like a centerpiece on the table. The purpose of having folks over isn't to show off an impressive environment. It's to get to know them better to see if we might connect in a way that points toward a meaningful friendship. If I start to get off track with this, I remember the final meal Jesus and His disciples shared together.

During the Last Supper, the meal Jesus had with His disciples the night before He was to die on the cross, we see Jesus investing in the people who shared a table with Him (Matthew 26:17–30). We read about how Jesus gave thanks for the food and drink before He and His friends ate and drank together. He shared conversation with them about hard things (the betrayal of a friend) and helpful things (the forgiveness of sins). That passage of Matthew shares that they sang together too.

But what it doesn't share is what the actual room looked like where they ate their meal. We don't know if it was dusty or clean, tidy or cluttered. We don't know if the room could've appeared in a version of *Israel Living* magazine or if it looked like a wild band of kiddos had run roughshod over the entire place.

What we *do* know is what was said and eaten. Whether in biblical times or today, what is said and eaten is what's remembered. Let *that* be the priority.

People

Myquillyn Smith wisely stated that there are three classifications of people you need to be mindful of with any gathering: your guests, yourself, and the people living within the walls of your home.[3]

First, of course, we want to think of our guests! We want to think about how we can welcome them and make them feel most at home. Before they come, I ask about any dietary preferences or restrictions and tailor the menu accordingly. And I'll often think of a few questions to ask, just in case I feel I need them during dinner. I do my level best to be a good listener who's mindful of any particular life event—happy or hard—that guests are going through. I do my best to let our company direct the conversation so they feel comfortable and at ease. I love to ask follow-up questions to the topics they bring up. At the same time, I like to keep a few questions in my pocket to ask if I feel it'd be a good time to ask them.

What I don't want to do is monopolize the conversation or repeatedly direct everything back to me or my family.

Second, we want to think of ourselves. For example, what are some main-dish meals we can get started or make ahead of time to save ourselves some labor later on? I like to set the table early too, because then I know everyone has silverware, napkins, and a glass of water. Usually, I set up my meals buffet style because I think that adds to the laid-back feel of the event. People are then free to go back for seconds as they'd like.

But in considering my own energy and bandwidth, I've often just ordered pizza for my guests. It doesn't get easier than that!

Finally, we want to be mindful of family members who live with us. I admit at times I've not done this well, as I've encouraged (ordered!) people in my house to help with pre-company prep work. And while there's nothing wrong with asking family members to help with preparations, I've learned that giving my people a heads-up about what I need goes a long way to encourage good moods. In Myquillyn's words, "Just giving them a simple reminder of what's happening and when and of any expectations you have of them can make a world of difference."[4] So I share any expectations a day or two before folks are coming over, and then those can be completed at each person's discretion. Through the years, I also learned to let them know how long they needed to be "on deck" for help while folks were at the house. When that time ended, they were welcome to skedaddle to their rooms or wherever else they wanted to be.

Stress Less, Connect More

Here are some ideas to consider for opening up your home to someone in a simple, nonstressful way:

- Invite folks over for dinner but keep the workload easy by following more of Myquillyn's wisdom. If you're hosting and like to cook, make only two things. Let the other dinner items come from either the store or your guests.[5] If you don't like to cook, consider making one thing (like a salad) and buying some ready-to-bake pizzas from a place like Papa Murphy's to serve for dinner!

- Invite folks over for a simple soup-and-bread dinner. I've done this at least a dozen times, and it's always a hit.
- Host a clean-out-the-fridge leftovers party with recent (I repeat, recent!) leftovers that everyone shares.
- Ask a potential friend if she'd like to come over for coffee and a treat.
- Host a dessert party where each person brings a dessert for everyone to share. (Shout-out to Rebecca for this idea!)
- Set up a firepit in the front yard and invite your neighbors to join you for conversation, s'mores, and hot chocolate.
- Set up a regular but rotating monthly calendar date to get together with a friend or friends for dinner at each other's homes.

Opening up our homes is the single biggest action we can take toward finding the friends we want to have. Inviting people into your home really does shorten the distance between another's heart and yours. If we open our homes, we open our hearts. And this opens us up to connection with people who are becoming our friends.

But if you come to my house, please leave the LEGO projects alone.

HOW TO BE A GOOD FRIEND

Inviting people into your home is the fastest way to encourage a friendship connection. But make it easy on yourself by remembering your boundaries, priorities, and the three categories of people to consider. (Thanks again, Myquillyn, for that wisdom!) When you welcome people into your home, you welcome them a bit further into your heart.

PART 3

WHAT A FRIEND WE HAVE IN JESUS

While Jesus knows what it feels like to be hurt and betrayed by friends, He's the only life-saving Friend who'll never let you down. And His own heart beats for you to have deep, life-giving friendships.

CHAPTER 21

MAKING FRIENDS BY PRAYING UP

Prayer lays hold of God's plan and
becomes the link between His will and its
accomplishment on earth. Amazing things
happen, and we are given the privilege of
being the channels of the Holy Spirit's prayer.
ELISABETH ELLIOT

Circa 2007, my husband informed me that he knew where the United States Air Force would be sending us next.

"We're going to Hawaii!" he said, a smile as big as Texas across his handsome face.

"ARE YOU SERIOUS?!" I hollered, staring at him. On the one hand, I was thrilled. I knew it would be a once-in-a-lifetime adventure for our family. On the other hand, I knew moving there meant I'd be thousands of miles from every soul I knew, family and friends. As a person whose lifeblood runs on relationships, that single fact outweighed all the heavenly beach scenes and island breezes.

As is typical for me, while conversing with my husband, I glossed over the good parts of Hawaii and went straight to my concerns. As is typical for my husband, he said in his carefree, unaffected way, "You'll make friends again, honey, just as you've done many times before."

I wasn't so sure. Certainly, Hawaii is paradise in its locational sense. As a beach-loving gal, I looked forward to that. But since we'd be living there and not just visiting on vacation, I wondered if it would feel as remote as it looked on a map. In fact, Hawaii is one of the most—if not *the* most—geographically remote island chains in the world. I spent no small amount of time fretting that moving there would make me isolated in friendships too.

And from a practical standpoint, just how many folks live on an island to make friends with in the first place? Plus, we were moving to the quieter island of Maui, not the more populated Oahu. While Maui is positively dreamy, my husband would be working at a detachment that was tiny compared to units at Pearl Harbor or Hickam Air Force Base on Oahu. Also, I'd heard stories that many folks weren't thrilled to have a military presence on the island in the first place. So I didn't have high hopes of finding friends there.

What's more, I carried a bit o' baggage from our previous assignment. Yes, I'd eventually made friends there, but it'd taken more than a year to do so—and that was with Olympic-sized pools of people to draw from. If it took me a long time to make friends in a large town surrounded by suburbs, surely it would take longer to make friends on an island.

From the moment we began packing up our house to the moment our plane touched down on the island, I prayed my everlovin' guts out. My repeat plea was, *Please, Lord, please let me make friends quicker than I did last time.*

After the long flight with three young children in tow, we finally landed in Kahului, Maui. The airport's open-air design immediately introduced us to the island's gentle trade winds. Though they were marvelously refreshing, I was plumb exhausted from managing three little ones on the flight.

Furthermore, even though I'd just set foot on the island, I already felt severely deficient in resources for the work it would take to get settled in a new place with a crop of new folks. Still, as we walked toward baggage claim, I prayed that God would make a way for solid friendships with others. And while I knew that God would answer my prayer in His timing, I also knew it would likely take a lot of time.

Throughout my life, whether regularly moving or staying put, I've prayed to find my people. God has never failed to answer that prayer, but how and when He answered it has varied as much as our mountain sunsets over the Rockies.

But I know now that when I'm faithful to keep praying, I'm placing myself in a better position to be on the lookout for ways He's answering that prayer.

God is no genie in a bottle, yet it's His will and His heart for you to have your people. When your longings align with His will for you, you can know He'll answer your prayer in the way you hope. Consider this passage from Ecclesiastes 4:9–10:

> Two are better than one,
> > because they have a good return for their labor:
> If either of them falls down,
> > one can help the other up.
> But pity anyone who falls
> > and has no one to help them up.

This is one example of many in the Bible where we're instructed to have friends and told why we need them. God communed with Moses (Exodus 33:11) and Abraham (James 2:23) as friends. Jesus' friends included Peter, James, and John, as well as Mary, Martha, and their brother, Lazarus. If our heavenly Father and His Son had friends, we know it's His will for us to have friends too.

Throughout John 14—16, Jesus stated four different times that if we pray in His name and in the Father's will, we can have what we ask for.

"I will do whatever you ask in my name, so that the Father may be glorified in the Son." (14:13)

"You may ask me for anything in my name, and I will do it." (14:14)

"If you remain in me and my words remain in you, ask whatever you wish, and it will be done for you." (15:7)

"Very truly I tell you, my Father will give you whatever you ask in my name." (16:23)

You and I will never, ever go wrong in praying for friends, because it's God's will for us to have friends. Therefore, He will answer that prayer by giving us friends. It may not happen as quickly as we'd like or with the people we thought we wanted to be friends with. But we can trust that as long as we're doing what we need to do to participate in the process, He will bring us the friends we need.

Praying in Jesus' name gives power to our words while connecting our own hearts to the Father's heart. We also have the

Holy Spirit, the third component of the triune God, who advocates for this very desire on your behalf and mine (John 14:16).

Prayer is a surefire way to take our eyes and attention off the problem of our loneliness and fix them on the One who gets us through our problems—the One who is indeed with us *in* our problems. When we participate in the process of finding friends by praying up along with showing up and opening up, we're positioning ourselves well to receive what God wants to give us. When we participate in the process, God will set us up for success by the power of the Holy Spirit.

Sometimes, I think we're praying for something we want, sure, but we're not praying like our lives depend on it. And really, given all the research about how a lack of friendships is catastrophic to our health, our lives *do* depend on it.

If I'm being no-holds-barred honest about my prayer life in the past, it's not been my strong suit. Speaker and author Jackie Hill Perry commented that the Lord spoke to her heart and said, "You are praying casually as if you need casual power. And you don't."[1] When I read that, I thought, *Same, Jackie. Same.* Sure, when a full-blown crisis befalls me, I'll get carpet fuzz up my nose from hours of my on-my-face praying. But until my move to Hawaii, I treated prayer with my friendships casually, not desperately. I didn't pray like it was a driving force toward meaningful communication and change.

But as I grew in my faith and learned just how important God views us having our people, I stopped praying like I thought it had no power. I stopped praying like I just wanted Him to nudge me in the direction of a potential friend. I began praying boldly that God would please, please, *please* bring some gals in my circumference whom I could connect with and who saw friendship potential in me. I stopped only tossing up the half-hearted request, *Lord, please bring me friends!* Instead, I started praying with serious, comprehensive, and detailed specifics. Some of those prayers have gone as follows:

- Lord, cross my path with a friend who has kids the same age as mine and can understand this challenging parenting season.
- Lord, cross my path with a friend who has kids older than mine so I can be encouraged in what's to come.
- Lord, give me wisdom in where and with whom to invest my time and resources so I can have a good return on my efforts. Show me who will reciprocate my friendship overtures with those of her own.
- Lord, if it's Your will, move the heart of (insert the name of a woman you've met whom you think would make a good friend) so she can see me as the potential friend I see her as being.
- Lord, if I'm looking in the wrong direction for friends, show me where I should look instead.
- Lord, as I go on this coffee date or to that dinner, please help our hearts connect. Help us both listen and respond in the way the other needs.
- Lord, open my eyes to someone at (insert the name of a place near you) who needs a friend, and help my heart to want to cultivate a friendship with her.
- Lord, show me places I can regularly show up to increase the odds of making a friendship connection with someone.
- Lord, give me wisdom about who to be wide-awake to and who to be wary of in terms of friendships. Help me know who to steer clear of and who to give the benefit of the doubt.
- Lord, help me do what I can to prevent a spirit of division in my friendships.

Another practice that helps me pray more seriously is journaling my prayers. And when I journal those prayers, I get *real* honest. As in, I say what I'm only comfortable saying to God.

My husband knows more about me than anyone. My best friend and closest circle of friends know most things about me. And yet, they don't know everything—only God does. In fact, those journals are so real and raw that when I pass away, I have a plan for them to be burned. I don't want a soul other than me reading them!

If you decide to take up this practice yourself, be prepared for God to give you some answers to the questions you have as you're praying. Be prepared for Him to give you insights into the circumstances you're praying about. Journaling won't magically clarify your path forward to finding a profusion of friends. But it *will* clarify your next small step. It won't magically remove the fog around your situation to make you see why, for example, you were ghosted by that woman who seemed interested in a friendship. But it will give you peace through the presence of Christ within the fog.

When I pray, I don't find that whatever storm I'm enduring is immediately calmed. But *I* am calmed within the storm.

Also, it does a heck of a lot of good to write those answers down and reflect on the legacy of God's faithfulness in your life. Journaling not only comforts you; it shows your future self all the ways God spoke to you and was there for you in the past. Therefore, you'd better believe He'll do so again.

I often think of prayer as a conversation with God, and this encourages me to leave room for Him to respond back to me. And that in turn leaves room for expectancy, for Him to answer my prayers in ways beyond what I could imagine.

That is what happened to me in Hawaii. I discovered that the Lord can grant us something above and beyond what we even think to ask of Him. From the very moment we arrived on the island—indeed, at the airport—God answered my prayer for friends swiftly and completely through Kim, the wife of David's commander. She and her husband were there to welcome us to the island, and they continued to welcome us by way of inviting us into their home.

What's more, they started the detachment-wide tradition of First Fridays. On the first Friday of each month, the whole detachment and their families met at the park and shared pizza and conversation. The adults had a chance to talk while the kids burned energy climbing trees and playing on the swing sets. These regularly scheduled events, as well as others, became reliable points of connection between other women and me. Kim knew the value of opening up and showing up, and because of that, God used her as the answer to my own praying up.

God answered my friendship worries before I even prayed, and He showed me how He can bring abundance anywhere. His limitless abilities to care for us aren't based on what we see in front of us—or what we don't see.

I love what C. S. Lewis wrote:

> In Friendship . . . we think we have chosen our peers. In reality, a few years' difference in the dates of our births, a few more miles between certain houses, the choice of one university instead of another, posting to different regiments, the accident of a topic being raised or not raised at a first meeting—any of these chances might have kept us apart. But, for a Christian, there are, strictly speaking, no chances. A secret Master of the Ceremonies has been at work.[2]

Prayer is how I set myself up to be in God's right place within His right timing, so I'm well positioned to receive His friendship blessing.

Because of Hawaii's remote island location, I assumed I'd struggle to make friends there. Yet God surprised me by promptly answering my prayers for friends. The Master of Ceremonies may be writing a longer story by making us wait for our friends, or He may be writing a shorter one. Either way, our current circumstances don't determine the end of the story. When we participate with Him through prayer, He will get us where we're supposed to be—and with whom. He is faithful to bring the story to a redeeming conclusion.

> Prayer is how I set myself up to be in God's right place within His right timing, so I'm well positioned to receive His friendship blessing.

Above all else, know that Jesus is your always faithful Friend who walks with you as you find your friends and grow your friendships.

WHAT A FRIEND WE HAVE IN JESUS

Prayer is how we activate participation with our Father in heaven so His will connects with what we receive. When we pray in Jesus' name, we infuse our prayers with power. It's God's will for you to have friends, so pray seriously and specifically to that end.

CHAPTER 22

THE FRIEND WHO NEVER
FAILS IN FRIENDSHIP

*What if you could have a friend who knew you
better than anyone, better than you even know
yourself? And what if, knowing everything, he
still loved you, and even liked you? . . . And
what if you could have a friend who, by his very
relationship with you, would transform you to
become a better friend to others? You can. His
name is Jesus. He's called the friend of sinners.*
DREW HUNTER, *MADE FOR FRIENDSHIP*

Not long ago, a friend of mine told me about a time when
her now-grown daughter was in high school and struggled
to connect with someone—anyone—in her church youth
group. While my friend's family had been a part of that church

since her daughter was in middle school, most of the other girls in the youth group had known each other since first or second grade. Every Sunday morning at church and Wednesday evening at youth group, my friend's daughter would try to engage one or more girls in conversation. She'd ask them questions or comment positively on something about them. And every time, she'd receive stiff, monosyllabic responses in return.

My friend felt frustrated on behalf of her daughter, but that frustration leveled up when, one Sunday, she watched from a distance how these girls treated her daughter.

Each Sunday, several girls from that youth group would sit together in church. Before the service started, my friend's daughter would walk over to the row and say hello to a couple of the girls sitting on the end. My friend watched as the two girls, barely raising their heads, tossed a weak hello her daughter's way before quickly looking down once again.

My friend then told me, "After observing their conduct, and watching my daughter walk away dejected yet again, I shook with rage. It was all I could do not to march over there myself, grab a girl or two by the hair, and tell them their rude behavior was *not* a good look and needed a 180-degree turn, *pronto*."

I've been tempted to do the same. I've wanted to shake a girl or two awake to their dialed-up offensive behavior. What's more, I've wanted to do the same with their parents. I've wanted to tell them in no uncertain terms, "Listen, we mamas and dads are all gonna miss things in our parenting. It happens. But it appears you've failed to cover 'Welcoming Outsiders and Interpersonal Kindness 101' in your own parenting. Unless I'm wrong, your child needs a refresher course yesterday."

Maybe that sounds harsh, and heaven knows my own parenting has gaping holes of its own. Still, I've seen this scenario play out toward members of my own family and with other families enough to know it's something that needs addressing. In the words of Drew Hunter, "Jesus invites us to expand his circle of fellowship. He sends us out to welcome others in."[1]

Whether our kids have their friends or not, and whether we have our friends or not, kids need to see us grown-ups normalizing the idea of reaching out to new people, not just following the familiar tracks to the people we already know.

Having said that, it's also true, as author Priya Parker wisely states, "If everyone is invited, no one is invited—in the sense of being truly held by [a] group."[2] Certainly, if everyone is invited, no one gets to enjoy the submarine benefits of deep connection. But for the love of all that's holy, we're never too busy or too important to offer a warm and welcoming, "Hello! It's so nice to see you!" That doesn't mean we become best friends with that person. It means we're friendly to that person.

Over time, my friend cried tears of heartbreak because her daughter wasn't received into her own church's youth group, of all places. I've not been warmly welcomed—or acknowledged—by people who profess to love Jesus, and I bet you haven't either at times. It's terribly difficult when any friend or potential friend fails us, of course. But it's salt in the wound when that friend is a Christian. Alas, Christians aren't immune to the reality of cliques—friend groups gone wrong through an air of exclusivity rather than availability.

C. S. Lewis wrote, "Friendship must exclude. From the innocent and necessary act of excluding to the spirit of exclusiveness is an easy step; and thence to the degrading pleasure of exclusiveness."[3]

We'll all run across friend groups we'd like to be a part of but can't. And whether that's due to cliquishness or some other reason, there are a million ways our friends may fail us. And if we're being honest, we may fail them.

But what we don't want to do is go from experiencing the failings of Christians—and our desire to turn tail from those folks—to turning away from Christ Himself. Because Jesus is the only Friend who will never, ever fail us.

This is true, but that doesn't mean we don't need friends. When Mary Magdalene came to the tomb the morning Jesus rose from the dead, she mistook Him for the gardener till Jesus said her name (John 20:16). We need friends because, indeed, God whispers our names through flesh-and-blood people.[4] He speaks to us through others in a thousand different ways.

Also, as Kristin Hill Taylor writes,

> God's communal nature is confirmed by the New and Old Testaments. God exists as Father, who loved us so much He sacrificed His only Son; Jesus, the Son of God who made a way for us to have access to the Father and showed us how to live; and the Spirit, who encourages, sanctifies, and advocates for us.[5]

God, who's in constant participation in the community of the Trinity, wants you to have community with Him and with other people. And while God's actions can change as He sees fit, His character never changes.[6] Charles Spurgeon said,

> Christ is "a friend that sticks closer than a brother." . . . You have often left him; has he ever left you? You have had many trials and troubles; has he ever deserted you? . . . No, children of God, it is your solemn duty to say "No," and bear witness to his faithfulness.[7]

Jesus, our Friend who loves us more than our most devoted families love us, is always supporting us in what we most need in our lives, including friendships.

But Jesus isn't just a true-blue-at-all-times Friend. He was and is the perfect Friend, and yet His own friends failed Him. He's walked in your shoes regarding rejection, ugliness, duplicity, slander, attempts to be manipulated, character assassination, and the overall failures you've experienced at the hands of your own friends. Jesus' disciple and friend Judas walked the highways and byways of life alongside Jesus. He soaked up Jesus' wisdom and friendship firsthand. And yet his profound betrayal of Jesus lives on in infamy (Matthew 26:14–18).

Jesus' hometown friends and family, after hearing Him preach a mini-sermon that hit too close to home for their liking, tried to throw Him over a literal cliff (Luke 4:24–30). Now, I've been hurt by friends, but I've never had my life threatened as a part of that. What's more, Jesus is the Friend who voluntarily walked over a cliff for you. Dane Ortlund, in his book *Gentle and Lowly*, writes, "Jesus came to the cliff of the cross and didn't change his mind. He walked over the edge."[8] Jesus didn't get pushed over the edge, and He didn't evade the edge. He walked over it so you and I could be kept a safe distance from it. He is your greatest ally, rescuer, and refuge. He calls you friend (John 15:15) and chosen (1 Thessalonians 1:4).

Any failing we've suffered because of our friends, Jesus looks us in the eye and says, "I get it, and I know exactly how you feel." And He means it.

But Jesus doesn't just empathize with us in our pain. He wants us to give Him all our pain. Those feelings and concerns are in good hands when placed in His hands. He'll deal with them for us.

Proverbs 1:33 says, "First pay attention to me, and then relax. Now you can take it easy—you're in good hands" (MSG). This verse reminds us that when we first tend to our friendship with our loving Savior, we'll find ourselves affirmed in who we are and *whose* we are. Even if we don't know why a friendship took the turn it did, we can relax because God *does* know. He wouldn't have allowed it to happen to us if it didn't bring about some future benefit for us.

Hebrews 11:1 says, "Faith is confidence in what we hope for and assurance about what we do not see." Faith isn't seeing. It's believing in spite of not seeing. Part of giving Jesus our feelings and struggles over friendship failings is saying, *I don't get this at all, but I believe You know best in spite of that.*

As Beth Moore writes, "Your greatest reality in your greatest difficulty is an invisible, all-powerful God."[9]

Jesus does not get overwhelmed by us, tired of us, or annoyed with us. He'll never reject us. Whatever we ask of Him, He has a bottomless capacity to meet our bottomless needs. That is what distinguishes Him from any friends walking alongside us on this planet.

In John 15:15–16, Jesus said, "I have called you friends, for everything that I learned from my Father I have made known to you. You did not choose me, but I chose you and appointed you so that you might go and bear fruit." Just as Jesus chose us, we get to choose our friends. But before we choose our friends, we have to make the choice to choose friends in the first place.

You can make that choice by choosing to spend your time being a good friend to yourself. You do that by accepting that making friends takes work, is dang hard, and is dang awkward. It will hold its fertilizer seasons, but that fertilizer is what eventually helps you grow a harvest of friendships. You remember that boundaries are your friends—and your friends' friends. So you're not afraid to use them, and you don't react when others use them too. You won't let rejection stop you from pursuing friendships. And you believe it's normal to endure seasons when finding friends takes longer than you'd like.

Also, you make that choice by choosing to spend your time being a good friend to others just the same. You do that by keeping reasonable expectations and giving grace (relaxing instead of reacting!) when others don't respond to your communication as quickly as you'd like. You look for ways to speak affectionately—to be another's hype girl—through verbal or written encouragement to your friends and potential friends. You activate the relational superpower that is celebrating another's successes. You look not only at women in your own life stage as potential friends but also at those further down the road from you as well as those coming up behind. You mourn the loss of friendships ending without your say-so, but you take comfort in the fact that the ending did have God's say-so. You own that rejection is very difficult, but it's a part of life, not the end of it. You take advantage of rituals that help you build your friendships by doing the thinking for you. You remember that you care more about keeping strong connections with friends than about airing strong opinions in an effort to be "correct." Finally, you don't throw away quality friendships. Instead, you regularly show up, open up, and pray up for your friends so you actively participate in the process of friendship.

If you're like me and have had to put in the work to make new friends in new places (or new seasons of life) over and over again, remember that with this commitment to try again to find the friends you need, you're not starting over. As I've learned from a couple of smart military spouses, you're starting from a place of experience.[10] You've learned a lot about making friends and why it's worth the effort, and eventually, the work you put in will feel like a more natural part of the rhythm of your days and your life.

And if you do lack the experience, don't worry one bit. None of us is an expert at things we're only just beginning to learn. The good news is, you have this book to get you moving in the right direction!

When we're fueled by Jesus' love for us, we'll naturally fret less about a lack of friends. As we set our hope in Him, we know He'll give us what we need. We can weather hard friend seasons when we're filled up with Christ, the only Friend who always loves best, cares most, and walks with us through all the ups and downs of friendships. He holds us during friendship heartbreak. He's with us as we work to make friends. And He will be faithful to see that we find them.

My friend's daughter from the beginning of this chapter didn't let the unfriendly youth group decide the ending of that story. She began attending a new youth group at a different church that wholeheartedly welcomed her, and her faith grew as she saw the faithfulness of God in people who modeled the love, acceptance, and friendship of Jesus. She reaped the rewards of trying again for the friendships she needed.

A few years ago, while still trying to find my Colorado people, I was kindly invited to the home of a fairly well-known author for an evening gathering. I showed up at her beautiful house not knowing anyone except for a friend who was also a friend of the author-host. After greeting the host and grabbing a small plate of delectable-looking goodies, I chatted with my friend before she had to leave. I made small talk with a couple of other folks as I collected a second macaron and a scoop of fancy nuts. Not finding any open seating within the rooms, I plopped myself down partway up the wide staircase to the home's second floor.

From that vantage point, I watched as several groups of twos and threes talked together, and I watched as another larger group moved as a clump around our gracious host. In my Desperate Era, I would've surveyed that scene from my lone spot on the stairs and immediately started to feel sorry for myself. From that place of insecurity, I would've thought, *Why can't I find anyone to talk with? What's wrong with me? I don't belong here!*

But now, as I munched on my snacks, I saw a different view. Not only that, I saw that view as a different person.

Then and now, whether I'm alone in a crowd or just plain alone, I don't let that turn me inward. I don't assume that a lack of outward signs of connection is a sign that something is wrong with me. I also don't let that turn me outward by comparing myself to others in the room. Instead, I turn upward and say, *God, thank You for the invitation to rub shoulders with others, even if I don't make a connection with anyone. Because I'm willing to put in the work on my end, I know You'll bring me my people. While there's nothing wrong with being desperate for friends, thank You that I don't have to react out of that desperation. Thank You that I can relax at peace here instead. While I wait to find the friends I need, thank You that Your presence always goes with me.*

When I look back on my friendship struggles—from being desperate enough to hold up a front-yard sign in search of friends to learning how to reach out to others to discovering that rejection is hard but won't kill me—I see how God has faithfully answered all my friendship needs, and Jesus has faithfully walked beside me and encouraged me through all my friendship failures and successes. I sense this in my past and present, so I can be secure in it for my future too.

Eventually, Jesus did bring me my friends. And if He could do that for me, a gal who didn't know a lick about how to make friends, He will bring you the friendships you need too.

Esther Edwards Burr, mother of early American leader Aaron Burr Jr., said, "Friendship . . . Tis the Life of Life."[11] If that wasn't true, we wouldn't feel a sense of desperation when we don't have them. But it's my prayer that after walking with me through these pages, your desperation will turn to action as you make healthy choices to be a good friend to yourself and others. May you always persevere past any rejection or dead ends you experience. And may the successes you inevitably enjoy show you that it's always worth it to try again for the friendships you need.

WHAT A FRIEND WE HAVE IN JESUS

Friends will fail us; Jesus is the only Friend who never will. God is with you as He goes to unimaginable lengths to get you the friends you're supposed to have, and Jesus is your living proof that this is true.

ACKNOWLEDGMENTS

This book is years in the organizing and writing, and it's a lifetime in the living and learning. One can't write a book on friendship unless other people are a part of the living and the learning, and I'm so thankful for each and every person who generously showed me grace and favor in the process.

To every porch friend and reader who has ever read anything I've written and in turn shared a bit of your own story with me, thank you for your generosity, trust, kindness, and support.

To Drew Hunter: You don't know me at all, but I got to know you, at least in part, through your tremendous book *Made for Friendship*. Thank you for writing it and offering it to those of us who want to experience friendship as God intended it.

To the entire team at W Publishing, including Lisa-Jo Baker, Stephanie Newton, Lauren Ash, Caren Wolfe, Elizabeth Hawkins, Rachel Buller, and Meg Schmidt: You can ask several people in my real life what I think of you, and they'd all tell you the same thing—you're a dream to work with, and I adore each of you. Thank you for believing in me and in this book's message, and thank you for making its message truly shine.

Lisa-Jo Baker, I've known you as a true-blue friend and whip-smart writer for over fifteen years, but what a delight it's been to get to know you as a bang-up editor too! Your eagle eye for details and wisdom for big-picture vision is a wonder to behold. I love you more than you love black tea and jacaranda trees.

To Retha and Kaitlyn: I wouldn't accomplish a lick without your help, direction, and encouragement. You are two of the dearest of the dear hearts, and I love you.

To Mary DeMuth: You're a literary agent who goes to the ends of the earth to encourage and educate your authors, and we're so much better at what we do because of what you do. Thank you for all you do to support me, guide me, and talk me off rooftops. You're simply marvelous.

To all the friends who so generously let me share their stories that were a part of my own, including Joe, JulieAnne, Aundrea, Aimée, Alli, Maria, Rebecca, and others still: Thank you doesn't even begin to cover it. Y'all are *the* best.

To my wingwomen, past and present, including Aimée, Alli, Aundrea, Cheryl, Christie, Connie, Holley, Jen B., Jen P., JulieAnne, Kathy, Lindsey, Lisa-Jo, Kim, Maria, Michelle, Rachel, Rebecca, Salena, as well as the Juniper bunch and the Emmanuel Lutheran Wednesday morning Bible study ladies: Thank you for seeing me through many a friendship season and for the gift of your friendship that saw me through many a difficult season.

To the Petersen, Leonard, and Crumpton families: I love you to pieces.

To the PAC gals and fellas: Thank you for being my framily and my family's framily.

To Aimée: Thank you for the endless, wholehearted encouragement on absolutely every subject under the sun. Life always looks and feels brighter and better after a good conversation with you. May the coffee dates live on and on!

To the O'Neill and Strong families: Thank you for all the ways you've supported my writing. Sara, Keri, Erin, Lisa, and

Bev, thank you for asking me about this project and for listening with enthusiasm.

James, Ethan, and Faith: Thank you for your interest, prayers, and timely "Way to go, Mama!" hurrahs when I reached a milestone in writing this book. I couldn't be prouder or more thrilled to be your mama! You'll always be my and your dad's priority blessings and the smartest, kindest, funniest people we know.

To my good fella, David: You're my steady anchor in all my changing friendship seasons. You're the best kind of friend in that way—in every way. What a bang-up gift it is to walk through life side by side with you. I love you so.

Thank you to my heavenly Father, and for the eternally faithful friendship of Your Son, Jesus. Without Him, I wouldn't have the friends I have today—or be the friend I've learned to be.

NOTES

Introduction

1. C. S. Lewis, *The Four Loves* (Harcourt, Brace, 1960), 57.
2. Dr. Timothy Keller, "Friendship," sermon, Gospel in Life, December 15, 2021, video, 32:03, https://podcast.gospelinlife .com/e/friendship-1639496383/.
3. Drew Hunter, *Made for Friendship: The Relationship That Halves Our Sorrows and Doubles Our Joys* (Crossway, 2018), 41.

Chapter 1: Title Explained: Making a Sign to Hold in My Front Yard

1. Daniel A. Cox, "The State of American Friendships: Change, Challenges, and Loss," Survey Center on American Life, June 8, 2021, https://www.americansurveycenter.org/research /the-state-of-american-friendship-change-challenges-and-loss/.
2. Data Team, "Parents Now Spend Twice as Much Time with Their Children as 50 Years Ago," *Economist*, November 27, 2017, https://www.economist.com/graphic-detail/2017/11/27 /parents-now-spend-twice-as-much-time-with-their-children -as-50-years-ago.
3. Arthur Brooks cited in Peter Attia, "Prioritizing 'Real Friends' over 'Deal Friends,'" *Peter Attia, MD* (blog), August 27, 2022, https://peterattiamd.com/real-friends-over-deal-friends/.
4. Attia, "Prioritizing 'Real Friends.'"
5. Matthias R. Mehl et al., "Eavesdropping on Happiness: Well-Being Is Related to Having Less Small Talk and More Substantive

Conversations," *Psychological Science* 21, no. 4 (2010): 539–41, www.ncbi.nlm.nih.gov/pmc/articles/PMC2861779/.

6. Lenny Bernstein, "U.S. Life Expectancy Declines Again, a Dismal Trend Not Seen Since World War I," *Washington Post*, November 29, 2018, https://www.washingtonpost.com /national/health-science/us-life-expectancy-declines-again -a-dismal-trend-not-seen-since-world-war-i/2018/11/28 /ae58bc8c-f28c-11e8-bc79–68604ed88993_story.html.

Chapter 2: It's Not Just You. Making Friends Is Hard.

1. Sally Clarkson (@sallyclarkson), "Teatime Tuesday," Instagram, January 3, 2023, https://www.instagram.com/p/Cm9Q7-SuEbw/.

2. Lysa TerKeurst, *Uninvited: Living Loved When You Feel Less Than, Left Out, and Lonely* (Nelson Books, 2016), 85.

Chapter 3: Don't Discount the Fertilizer Seasons

1. Julie Weisenhorn and Natalie Hoidal, "Ask Extension: Do Fertilizers Help or Hurt Plants?" University of Minnesota Extension, March 23, 2021, https://extension.umn.edu /yard-and-garden-news/ask-extension-do-fertilizers-help -or-hurt-plants.

2. "Aged Manure," Dutch Style Landscaping, accessed June 30, 2024, https://dutchstylelandscaping.ca/aged-manure/.

3. Nikki Tilley, "The Benefits of Manure Compost in Your Gardening," Gardening Know-How, June 1, 2021, https://www.gardeningknowhow.com/composting/manures /the-benefits-of-manure-in-your-garden.htm.

4. Bonnie Gray, personal email communication to the author, January 10, 2023.

Chapter 4: Get Cozy and Comfortable with Awkward

1. Noor Bouzidi, "How Do I Make Friends Now?" *The Cut*, November 9, 2021, 3:20, https://www.thecut.com/2021/11/the -cut-podcast-how-do-i-make-friends-now.html.

Chapter 5: Boundaries Are Your Friends

1. Chrystal Hurst, "Session Three: Better Together, Unity, How to Love & Disagree," (in) Real Life FRIENDED Lifeway Live event, Nashville, October 14, 2017.
2. Gary Thomas, *When to Walk Away: Finding Freedom from Toxic People* (Zondervan, 2019), 142.
3. Kaitlyn Bouchillon, "You Are Not a Trash Can," (in)courage, October 14, 2022, https://www.incourage.me/2022/10/you-are-not-a-trash-can.html.
4. Bouchillon, "You Are Not a Trash Can."

Chapter 6: Boundaries Are Your Friends' Friends

1. Nedra Tawwab (@nedratawwab), "Ways you might be violating other people's boundaries," Instagram, February 15, 2024, https://www.instagram.com/p/C3X3DW3sryY/.
2. Tawwab, "Ways you might be violating other people's boundaries."
3. Beth Moore, *Whispers of Hope: 10 Weeks of Devotional Prayer* (B&H, 2013), 121.
4. Quoted in Bruce Y. Lee, "How to Tell Friends for Life from Friends for a Reason or a Season," *A Funny Bone to Pick* (blog), *Psychology Today*, July 6, 2023, https://www.psychologytoday.com/us/blog/a-funny-bone-to-pick/202306/how-to-tell-a-friend-for-life-versus-a-reason-or-a-season.

Chapter 7: Believe in Surprise Friendships

1. "Jordan River," BibleCharts.org, accessed September 18, 2024, https://www.biblecharts.org/biblelandnotes/Jordan%20River.pdf; "How Wide and Deep Was the Jordan River Where Israel Crossed?" NeverThirsty, accessed September 18, 2024, https://www.neverthirsty.org/bible-qa/qa-archives/question/wide-deep-jordan-river-israel-crossed/.

2. Priscilla Shirer, *Awaken: 90 Days with the God Who Speaks* (B&H, 2017), 312.

Chapter 8: When Finding Friends Takes Forever, Ask Yourself These Questions

1. Drew Hunter, *Made for Friendship: The Relationship That Halves Our Sorrows and Doubles Our Joys* (Crossway, 2018), 26.
2. Timothy Keller, *The Reason for God: Belief in an Age of Skepticism* (Viking, 2008), 193–94.
3. Joni Eareckson Tada (@joniandfriends), "God permits what he hates to accomplish what he loves," Instagram video, March 2, 2024, https://www.instagram.com/p/C4BF4wRr0vm/.

Chapter 9: What You Can Expect Will Kill Your Friendships

1. Ann Voskamp, *One Thousand Gifts: A Dare to Live Fully Right Where You Are* (Zondervan, 2010), 169.
2. Drew Hunter, *Made for Friendship: The Relationship That Halves Our Sorrows and Doubles Our Joys* (Crossway, 2018), 102.
3. C. S. Lewis, *Letters of C. S. Lewis* (Harcourt, 1966), 429.

Chapter 10: Pioneer Up

1. Faith, my darling twenty-one-year-old daughter, if you're reading this, have more empathy for us than I had for my parents, because, indeed, *I was very young*.
2. Annie F. Downs, "Episode 184: Kristen Strong," *That Sounds Fun*, podcast, 33:30, accessed December 23, 2024, https://www.anniefdowns.com/podcast/episode-184-kristen-strong/.
3. Lindsey Phillips, "The Emotional and Social Health Needs of Gen Z," American Counseling Association, January 2022, https://www.counseling.org/publications/counseling-today-magazine/article-archive/article/legacy/the-emotional-and-social-health-needs-of-gen-z.

Chapter 11: Tell People What You Think of Them (No, Really)

1. University of Utah study, cited in Teddy Amenabar, "Want to Be Healthier? Hang Out with Your Friends," *Washington Post*, updated February 12, 2024, https://www.washingtonpost.com /wellness/2023/01/09/how-to-adult-friends-relationships /?utm_source=instagram&utm_medium=social&utm _campaign=wp_main&crl8_id=15856b2e-45cd-49ec -94d5-398eacc03cf3.

2. For other friends interested in this recipe as well, it's in Bri McKoy's *The Cook's Book* (Revell, 2023). Yum!

3. Will Guidara, *Unreasonable Hospitality: The Remarkable Power of Giving People More Than They Expect* (Penguin Random House, 2022), 70.

4. Dr. Timothy Keller, "Spiritual Friendship," sermon, Redeemer Presbyterian Church, June 1, 2008, shared on *Gospel in Life*, podcast, November 23, 2022, https://podcast.gospelinlife.com /e/spiritual-friendship/.

5. Leslie Bennet Smith, "Ode to the Epistolary," *Victoria*, January/ February 2024, 53, 60.

6. Guidara, *Unreasonable Hospitality*, 28.

Chapter 12: *Freudenfreude* Is Your Relational Superpower

1. *New York Times* (@nyt_well), "Freudenfreude," Instagram, December 2, 2022, https://www.instagram.com/p /ClrMSvuOGtj/.

2. @nyt_well, "Freudenfreude."

3. Juli Fraga, "The Opposite of Schadenfreude Is Freudenfreude. Here's How to Cultivate It," *New York Times*, updated November 28, 2022, https://www.nytimes.com/2022/11/25/well /mind/schadenfreude-freudenfreude.html.

4. Fraga, "The Opposite of Schadenfreude Is Freudenfreude."

5. Fraga.

6. Fraga.

7. Kari Kampaki, *10 Ultimate Truths Girls Should Know* (Thomas Nelson, 2014), 12.

Chapter 13: The Benefits of Bookend Friends

1. Lauren Ramons, "Friendship and Mentorship," Mentor Collective, July 21, 2022, https://www.mentorcollective.org/blog /friendship-and-mentorship#:~:text=Friendship%20offers %20a%20level%20of,creates%20nuance%20within%20each %20role.
2. Dr. Timothy Keller, "Friendship," sermon, Redeemer Presbyterian Church, May 29, 2005, shared on *Gospel in Life*, podcast, December 15, 2021, 14:42, https://podcast.gospelinlife .com/e/friendship-1639496383/.
3. Keller, "Friendship," 12:20.
4. Keller, 13:52.

Chapter 14: When a Friendship Ends Without Your Say-So

1. Drew Hunter, *Made for Friendship: The Relationship That Halves Our Sorrows and Doubles Our Joys* (Crossway, 2018), 102.
2. Savannah Guthrie, *Mostly What God Does: Reflections on Seeking and Finding His Love Everywhere* (W Publishing, 2024), 8.
3. Phylicia Masonheimer, *Every Woman a Theologian*, email newsletter, June 10, 2024.

Chapter 15: Rejection Sucks, but Don't Let It Suck You Down

1. Anjuli Paschall (@lovealways.anjuli), "I've been through a handful of friendship break ups," Instagram, June 12, 2023, https://www.instagram.com/p/CtaQSzNpYcj/.
2. Melanie Shankle, "Patreon Episode with Melanie Shankle and Sophie Hudson," February 25, 2022, *Big Boo Cast*, podcast, 47:10, https://www.patreon.com/posts/february-2022–62873705.
3. Email communication with the author.
4. Nicole Zasowski (@nicolezasowski), "3 Reasons We Might

Remain Emotionally Stuck in Our Pain," Instagram, March 14, 2024, https://www.instagram.com/p/C4f0VeUrd9y/.

5. Thank you to my friend Allison for making this profound point to me in a conversation!

6. Lucretia Berry, in (in)courage, *100 Days of Strength in Any Struggle: A Devotional Journal* (DaySpring, 2024), day 26.

7. Brené Brown, quoted by Raising Potential (@raising_potential), "Know your worth," Instagram video, November 3, 2023, https://www.instagram.com/p/CzNkqt7ISDK/.

Chapter 16: Your Top-Notch Tool for Building Your Friendships

1. Rafael Nadal and John Carlin, *Rafa* (Hachette Books, 2020), 14.

2. Erica Bauermeister, "The Rituals of Winter," *Victoria,* December 2022, 13.

3. Will Guidara, *Unreasonable Hospitality* (Penguin Random House), 217.

4. Bethany Morris, "The Power of Rituals for Wellbeing," Peaceful Mind Psychology, June 4, 2023, https://peacefulmind.com.au /2023/04/06/the-rich-benefits-of-rituals/.

5. Drew Hunter, *Made for Friendship: The Relationship That Halves Our Sorrows and Doubles Our Joys* (Crossway, 2018), 102.

Chapter 17: I Love My friend to Pieces, but I Don't Love Her View on _____

1. Phylicia Masonheimer and Pricelis Perreaux-Dominguez, *Decision 2024: Unity and Dignity* (2024), 6.

2. C. S. Lewis, *The Four Loves* (Harcourt, Brace, 1960), 66.

3. Lewis, *The Four Loves*, 84.

4. Dominic Done, *Your Longing Has a Name: Come Alive to the Story You Were Made For* (W Publishing, 2022), 165.

5. Rachel Paula Abrahamson, "Inappropriate? Or Stunning? The Internet Is Heated over This Mother-of-the-Bride Dress,"

TODAY, June 11, 2024, https://www.today.com/parents/moms
/internet-divided-over-mother-bride-dress-rcna156403.

6. Oswald Chambers, "Getting There," *My Utmost for His Highest*
(Discovery House, 1992), June 11.

Chapter 18: Leave Room for Mistakes

1. Pope Francis, quoted in Courtney Mares, "Pope Frances
Decries Culture That 'Throws Away' Unborn Children,
Elderly, Poor," Catholic News Agency, January 29, 2023,
https://www.catholicnewsagency.com/news/253492/pope
-francis-decries-culture-that-throws-away-unborn-children
-elderly-poor.

2. Jennifer Rothschild, posted by Lifeway Women (@lifewaywomen),
"We say grace in the way we live to each other," Instagram video,
April 4, 2023, https://www.instagram.com/p/CqncOeaDY3g/.

3. Evelina Zaragoza Medina, "86 'Ted Lasso' Lines That Might
Make You Laugh, Cry, or Do Both Simultaneously," BuzzFeed,
updated September 17, 2024, https://www.buzzfeed.com
/evelinamedina/ted-lasso-best-quotes-jokes.

Chapter 19: Making Friends by Showing Up

1. Holley Gerth, "For the One Saying, 'I Should Have Known,'"
Holley Gerth (blog), video, 1:04, https://holleygerth
.thinkific.com/courses/take/heal/texts/51605671
-introduction-today-s-lesson-healing-step.

2. Olivia Singh, "John Krasinski Almost Quit Acting 3 Weeks
Before Landing His Role on *The Office*," *Business Insider*,
September 5, 2018, https://www.businessinsider.com
/john-krasinski-almost-quit-acting-before-landing-the
-office-role-video-2018-9.

3. National Theater Institute, "John Krasinski on Training at the
National Theater Institute," Facebook video, 0:24, August 24,
2016, https://www.facebook.com/NationalTheaterInstitute
/videos/10154064146603075/.

4. Outstanding Screenplays (@outstanding.screenplays), "John Krasinski Almost Quit Acting," Instagram video, August 28, 2023, https://www.instagram.com/p/CwgOIsEqePO/.

5. Singh, "John Krasinski Almost Quit Acting."

6. @outstanding.screenplays, "John Krasinski."

7. Jeffrey A. Hall, "How Many Hours Does It Take to Make a Friend?," *Journal of Social and Personal Relationships* 36, no. 4 (2019): 1286–92.

8. Email communication with the author, December 31, 2022.

9. Going Beyond and Priscilla Shirer (@_goingbeyond), "His ways are not our ways," Instagram video, January 26, 2024, https://www.instagram.com/p/C2kmFqDrAq1/.

Chapter 20: Making Friends by Opening Up

1. Priya Parker, *The Art of Gathering: How We Meet and Why It Matters* (Riverhead, 2018), 8.

2. Myquillyn Smith, *Welcome Home: A Cozy Minimalist Guide to Decorating and Hosting All Year Round* (Zondervan, 2020), 96–97, 148–49.

3. Smith, *Welcome Home*, 148–49.

4. Smith, 149.

5. Myquillyn Smith, "Hosting Part One: The Mood & the Food," *House Rules with Myquillyn Smith*, podcast, episode 10, November 9, 2023, transcript available at https://thenester.com/podcast/episode-10.

Chapter 21: Making Friends by Praying Up

1. Jackie Hill Perry, posted by Better Together TV (@bettertogethertv), "Prayer is vital to our walk with the Lord," Instagram video, September 26, 2023, https://www.instagram.com/p/CxqJWwEr06F/.

2. C. S. Lewis, *The Four Loves* (Harcourt, Brace, 1960), 89.

Chapter 22: The Friend Who Never Fails in Friendship

1. Drew Hunter, *Made for Friendship: The Relationship That Halves Our Sorrows and Doubles Our Joys* (Crossway, 2018), 155.

2. Priya Parker, *The Art of Gathering: How We Meet and Why It Matters* (Riverhead, 2018), 38.

3. C. S. Lewis, *The Four Loves*, (Harcourt, Brace, 1960), 85–86.

4. Dominic Done, *Your Longing Has a Name: Come Alive to the Story You Were Made For* (W Publishing, 2022), 162.

5. Quoted in Kristen Strong, comp., *Praying Through Loneliness: A 90-Day Devotional for Women* (W Publishing, 2024), 26.

6. Beth Moore, *Whispers of Hope* (B&H, 2013), 112.

7. Charles H. Spurgeon, "Sermon I: A Faithful Friend," in *Sermons of the Rev. C. H. Spurgeon*, 3d series (Sheldon, Blakeman, 1857), 13, 14.

8. Dane Ortlund, *Gentle and Lowly: The Heart of Christ for Sinners and Sufferers* (Crossway, 2020), 197.

9. Moore, *Whispers of Hope*, 109.

10. Wives of the Armed Forces (@wivesofthearmedforces), "Whether this is your 1st or 18th PCS," Instagram video, February 20, 2024, https://www.instagram.com/p/C3ksDQfskDB/.

11. Quoted in Justin Taylor, "Five Lessons on Friendship from Esther Edwards Burr," blog post, Gospel Coalition, June 18, 2013, https://www.thegospelcoalition.org/blogs/justin-taylor/fiv-lessons-on-friendship-from-esther-edwards-burr/.

ABOUT THE AUTHOR

KRISTEN STRONG, whose authored books include *Girl Meets Change* and *Friends Are Family We Choose*, also compiled the ninety-day devotional *Praying Through Loneliness*. She writes as the friend wanting to help you be the friend you want to have. She loves sharing laughs, long talks, and meaningful stories with family and friends while holding a cup of strong black tea. She and her US Air Force veteran husband, David, have three beloved adult children. Together this military family zigzagged across the country (and one ocean) several times before settling in Colorado Springs, Colorado. You can find her at kristenstrong.com, DaySpring's (in)courage, and on Instagram @kristenstrong.

Praying
Through
Loneliness

*a 90-day devotional
for women*

COMPILED BY
KRISTEN STRONG

In this devotional, take comfort in the vulnerable, personal stories from more than forty women who share their honest experiences of feeling isolated, struggling to find friends, and still finding a meaningful way through.

 W PUBLISHING GROUP